ASPEN PUBLISHERS

THE LEADERSHIP MATRIX: ELEMENTS OF EFFECTIVE LEADERSHIP

By: Jeffrey Hugh Newman, Esq.

Wolters Kluwer
Law & Business

Published by Wolters Kluwer Law & Business in New York.

Wolters Kluwer Law & Business serves customers worldwide with CCH, Aspen Publishers and Kluwer Law International products.

Printed in the United States of America

2 3 4 5 6 7 8 9 0

Library of Congress Cataloging-in-Publication Data

Newman, Jeffrey Hugh.
The leadership matrix : elements of effective leadership / by Jeffrey Hugh Newman, Esq.
p. cm.
Includes bibliographical references and index.
ISBN 978-1-4548-2166-3 (alk. paper)
1. Practice of law—United States. 2. Leadership—United States. I. Title.
KF300.N49 2012
340.068'4—dc23

2012025875

About Wolters Kluwer Law & Business

Wolters Kluwer Law & Business is a leading global provider of intelligent information and digital solutions for legal and business professionals in key specialty areas, and respected educational resources for professors and law students. Wolters Kluwer Law & Business connects legal and business professionals as well as those in the education market with timely, specialized authoritative content and information-enabled solutions to support success through productivity, accuracy and mobility.

Serving customers worldwide, Wolters Kluwer Law & Business products include those under the Aspen Publishers, CCH, Kluwer Law International, Loislaw, Best Case, ftwilliam.com and MediRegs family of products.

CCH products have been a trusted resource since 1913, and are highly regarded resources for legal, securities, antitrust and trade regulation, government contracting, banking, pension, payroll, employment and labor, and healthcare reimbursement and compliance professionals.

Aspen Publishers products provide essential information to attorneys, business professionals and law students. Written by preeminent authorities, the product line offers analytical and practical information in a range of specialty practice areas from securities law and intellectual property to mergers and acquisitions and pension/benefits. Aspen's trusted legal education resources provide professors and students with high-quality, up-to-date and effective resources for successful instruction and study in all areas of the law.

Kluwer Law International products provide the global business community with reliable international legal information in English. Legal practitioners, corporate counsel and business executives around the world rely on Kluwer Law journals, looseleafs, books, and electronic products for comprehensive information in many areas of international legal practice.

Loislaw is a comprehensive online legal research product providing legal content to law firm practitioners of various specializations. Loislaw provides attorneys with the ability to quickly and efficiently find the necessary legal information they need, when and where they need it, by facilitating access to primary law as well as state-specific law, records, forms and treatises.

Best Case Solutions is the leading bankruptcy software product to the bankruptcy industry. It provides software and workflow tools to flawlessly streamline petition preparation and the electronic filing process, while timely incorporating ever-changing court requirements.

ftwilliam.com offers employee benefits professionals the highest quality plan documents (retirement, welfare and non-qualified) and government forms (5500/PBGC, 1099 and IRS) software at highly competitive prices.

MediRegs products provide integrated health care compliance content and software solutions for professionals in healthcare, higher education and life sciences, including professionals in accounting, law and consulting.

Wolters Kluwer Law & Business, a division of Wolters Kluwer, is headquartered in New York. Wolters Kluwer is a market-leading global information services company focused on professionals.

WOLTERS KLUWER LAW & BUSINESS SUPPLEMENT NOTICE

This product is updated on a periodic basis with supplements to reflect important changes in the subject matter. If you have purchased this product directly from Wolters Kluwer Law & Business, we have already recorded your subscription for the update service.

If, however, you purchased this product from a bookstore and wish to receive future updates and revised or related volumes billed separately with a 30-day examination review, please contact our Customer Service Department at 1-800-234-1660 or send your name, company name (if applicable), address, and the title of the product to:

Wolters Kluwer Law & Business
Distribution Center
7201 McKinney Circle
Frederick, MD 21704

Important Contact Information

- To order any title, go to *www.aspenpublishers.com* or call 1-800-638-8437.
- To reinstate your manual update service, call 1-800-638-8437.
- To contact Customer Service, e-mail *customer.service@wolterskluwer.com,* call 1-800-234-1660, fax 1-800-901-9075, or mail correspondence to: Order Department—Aspen Publishers, Wolters Kluwer Law & Business, PO Box 990, Frederick, MD 21705.
- To review your account history or pay an invoice online, visit *www.aspenpublishers.com/payinvoices.*

Wolters Kluwer
Law & Business

TABLE OF CONTENTS

ACKNOWLEDGMENTS

The first acknowledgment belongs to the Creator . . . my books have been "in me" for years, but He allowed me the pleasure and fulfillment of sharing it with others. This has given me the opportunity to make an impression on the lives of others, howsoever insignificant. To allow me to feel that I am somehow giving back . . . I will always be grateful.

I thank the many people who have made an imprint on my life. I have been blessed. My first wife, Linda, who is one of the kindest people I know. My second wife, Sheryl, who died from cancer. She was one of the most graceful persons I have yet to know. She brought out the best in everyone she touched.

My parents, Mark and Gloria, my brother, Mark, and my children, Alyssa and Jon, each of whom, in entirely different ways, have had varying positive impacts on my growth and development.

Rabbi Pinsky of Temple Beth Torah, whose High Holiday sermon about crossword puzzles was the basis for an entire chapter in one book.

Mark Levick, who gave me the entry door to the International Council of Shopping Centers, a wonderful trade association, which became the springboard for my career in real estate.

Michael Kercheval and his incredible staff at the International Council of Shopping Centers, all of whom trusted me, and trust me to participate as a speaker at many of their events and as a leader of several committees.

Patricia Karetsky, who catalyzed me to start writing by advising it only requires an hour a day, and Ron Pompei, who constantly assured me that I had something worthwhile to communicate.

Victoria Wright, who constantly challenged me to write better, make my work clearer, make it "sing."

All of my friends and colleagues, who, in a variety of everyday little ways, helped me to grow, learn to laugh with myself, accept myself and appreciate myself.

Steven Gross, Chairman of my law firm, who has been both a friend and mentor, not just to me, but to all of my partners. Max Crane, Managing

Partner of my law firm, for his continuing support of my efforts in creating my books. Both true leaders.

Sonali Oberg, a Wolters Kluwer-Aspen Publishers Product Manager and jewel, who always believed in me. Ken Litt, my editor, who has made this process seamless.

I am especially thankful to all of my muses. How lucky and grateful am I to have multiple muses. My friend and significant other, Barbara. My colleague, Marcia, my terrific former assistant, Celeste, and my terrific current assistant, Carolyn.

Special thanks to my super motivators for whom leadership will be an uphill never-ending challenge . . . my grandchildren, Lia, Ari, Aviva and Eli.

Lastly, to all those who have come before me with leadership and other motivational works. I seek not to stand on their shoulders; rather, to some day perhaps stand shoulder-to-shoulder.

INTRODUCTION

THE LEADERSHIP MATRIX: Elements of Effective Leadership

Many books, articles, and essays on leadership seem fuzzy and ethereal. They are. They are because they only describe leadership successes, but fail to explain the "in the trenches" techniques used by successful leaders.

The following chapters meld the leadership concepts discussed by many and convert them into day-to-day kinetic interfaces between leaders and subordinates.

Many leadership techniques infuse the chapters that follow, but an overarching theme is either implied or, from time to time, expressed. The theme, in short, is avoidance or, at least, submersion, of a leader's ego. Egotude is simply overthinking any situation solely from one's personal perspective.

When we are overlooked and not included in a multi-recipient e-mail or a multi-attendee meeting, our ego, if unleashed, boils up as egotude. We may think, "How could they exclude me?," or "Why was Sally included but not me?," or "Don't they realize how important I am?," or perhaps worse yet, "Let them discuss it without me—who cares if they fail."

On the other hand, with our ego securely zipped up in our pocket, we might think, "They simply forgot to exclude me—probably just an oversight" or, better yet, "They must have had good reasons to exclude me—I'll find out why, if it's important, at a later time; for now, let me put my head 100% back into my work."

Which thought process do you think will likely cause indigestion? Which thought process will likely create a festering which, if not checked, may become the springboard for an outburst of anger or sarcasm—or worse—that should never have been said? An outburst we wish we could take back?

Just like the rest of us, effective leaders always struggle to control their ego, to put their insecurities to rest and focus on their primary goal. The primary goal of an effective leader is to facilitate the growth of all subordinates and align their improvement with the development and direction of the organization. The more effective the leader, the more subordinates are aligned with the evolution and direction of the organization.

Effective leaders understand that every subordinate is a "one-off." By definition, while we all have a similar psychological matrix, each person's fears, needs, desires, and talents manifest themselves differently. Hence, effective leaders mentor their "captains" who can devote the one-on-one mentoring to their lieutenants. In turn, lieutenants mentor their sergeants, and so on. Of course, effective leaders also know when to reach into the ranks to directly mentor subordinates with special potential, and how to do so without showing undue favor.

Effective leaders should recognize, as Socrates said, "I am human, nothing human is foreign to me." They recognize that from time to time their actions may be too self-serving, even selfish. But, they reflect—they think through the root cause and in so doing, they can remain more vigilant to avoid the self-sabotage of ego. They also recognize the shortcomings of others and, as will be seen in later chapters, use techniques to help the subordinate overcome or ameliorate the anxiety that, if unchecked, will exacerbate weaknesses and foibles and reduce the subordinate's performance level.

Effective leaders know that the only constant of a successful organization is change. The need to adapt is ever-present. Hence, the need to effectively communicate is critical. In a constantly evolving organizational dynamic, the bedrock must be clarity of communication.

Yet, how can the leader be certain that the communication is being heard and absorbed exactly as the leader intended? Perhaps 100% effective communication can never be achieved. Nevertheless, a good leader can achieve a sufficient level of understanding by utilizing the techniques in the chapters that follow.

I invite readers to reinforce what they already recognize is effective, and develop the techniques that follow in a manner that meshes with their particular personality to become even more effective.

We can only graduate from being merely a leader to being a truly effective leader by remaining on the lookout for the tremors of our egos. Catch them before they fester into an earthquake. We all must calm our internal tectonic plates so the waters of trespass by others do not seep in and disturb the crevices, but are allowed to harmlessly wash away.

Chapter 1

LEADERSHIP AND RED WINE

Effective leadership requires patience and mastery of the skill of listening. One is a developed trait; the other, an acquired skill. Yet, both are constantly subject to the dual sabotage of the demands of our customers and clients, exacerbated by the time starvation of our schedules.

Effective leaders recognize that a failure of patience and/or a failure to really listen always impairs the quality of their leadership. Why? Because successful leaders can create better strategies, and execute more effective plans to implement their strategies (or a more confident strategy or plan, even if not more effective), when they have more facts to analyze and synthesize.

For example, surely the lawyer who has more facts—whether about his client, his adversary's client, or his adversary—is in a better position to understand the strengths and weaknesses of the transaction or litigation he needs to analyze. Moreover, successful leaders recognize that much of the information they need cannot be obtained firsthand. It must be gleaned from colleagues, who may be senior, equal, or subordinate in the organization's hierarchy of power, influence, or ability.

Therefore, let's analyze one of the most typical fact-gathering interactions a leader encounters—the report by the subordinate working with the leader on a particular matter. Perhaps you are a mid-level or senior associate or a junior partner. It doesn't matter. In the report context, we are all leaders in the dynamic of those who report to us.

In order to be successful in the leadership role, we need to obtain all the information available. We need to constantly work to avoid the seven deadly words that reflect a failure of leadership—the seven words which erode, impale, or doom a strategy: "Why didn't you tell me that before?" These words indicate that we are inwardly or outwardly blaming another for the lack of disclosure, the failure to furnish all the essential information that was available at the time. However, successful leaders know the blame truly rests with them. We failed to obtain all the information available at the time. What could we have done, or should we have done differently, so that we obtained all the information then available?

Let's first look at a typical interaction between a subordinate about to deliver a report and the team leader to whom he is reporting. Let's assume you ask your junior associate to stop by your office to discuss the Jones matter, a matter both of you have been working on together for several months. You like this associate, but you would have preferred a more senior associate or simply a brighter associate to have been assigned to your team to assist in the matter.

What might you do to assure the quality of the report is diminished and the benefit of the meeting is minimally productive? Let's see. You could:

- constantly interrupt,
- make intentional or unintentional facial gestures of disdain, disinterest, or disbelief,
- read and, even worse, respond to your e-mails during the meeting,
- fidget with a ruler, paper clip, retractable pen, or other desk item,
- start grilling your associate before he is finished,
- quickly change the direction or subject of the meeting before your associate finishes.

But what should you do? In fact, what should you always do? Just be patient and listen carefully. Listen to what your associate is really trying to communicate—listen and really work to understand.

Perhaps you are thinking your associate knows how busy you are and how valuable your time is (that's your ego's attempt to sabotage the meeting). Of course your associate knows how busy you are and how valuable your time is! Those very thoughts constitute half of the ingredients for an unsuccessful report. The ingredients constituting the other half? Your associate's preference to focus only on the good news—all that he has accomplished and perhaps how difficult it was to accomplish it. Yet, the good news—which, of course, needs to be appreciated—often pales in significance to any bad news that never gets raised or thoroughly discussed. How can that happen? Why does it happen? How do we conduct ourselves to avoid the seven deadly words of leadership failure? How often have we thought or spoken those words in an even more important context, the all-too-often-after-the-fact conversation with our child when we have just learned—perhaps from a teacher or a neighbor, or by letter—that our child is failing, or has failed, in a subject or has received an incomplete, or is hanging out with the wrong crowd, or worse?

Think of your associate (your child, your spouse, your parent) as a bottle of very expensive red wine. You know—the good stuff that is bottled with a cork and has a dimple at the base of the bottle. So, you ask, what does a bottle of good red wine got to do with it?

Lots. Let's open a bottle together and share the experience. First, the initial sips taste good but get even better as the wine is exposed to the air. Second, we know that the sediment—oenologists call it the "lee"—has sunk and kind of attached to the bottom of the bottle. Similarly, after subordinates begin to speak, they usually speak more openly. They get more comfortable because we haven't cut them off and we haven't belittled them, intentionally or not. We simply avoided the actions set forth above; the actions that intimidate and demean. But, most important, we can't overlook what we know about every bottle of good red wine. The sediment is at the bottom. In other words, the stuff our associates won't be comfortable telling us—the mistake, the request for an extension that shouldn't have been needed, the missed fact—won't likely be revealed until we get near or at the bottom of the bottle (read: near or at the end of their report). Often, it's only after we've let them speak without demeaning interruption or negative non-verbal jabs that they, just like a good bottle of wine, really open up. Why? Because by letting them speak, they sense that we are working to really listen, and that we respect what they have to say. Our respect, our desire to understand, permeates the meeting like the bouquet from a bottle of good wine. In turn, that desire to understand, *i.e.*, our respect for them, converts into their comfort with and trust in us. As their comfort and trust increases, they become more likely to expose the sediment, or at least allow us to probe for it if they are unable to recognize it themselves.

Isn't that the way every interaction ought to be conducted? Isn't that exactly how people we really admire conduct themselves? They stop what they are doing and really listen to us when we seek their advice, no matter how busy or important we perceive them to be. If our leaders don't do that, are they really effective leaders? Okay, so we're all stressed, we don't think what the other person had to say will be anything more than a waste of our time—blah, blah, blah! The stress is almost always our ego (telling us we are simply too important). As for the meeting being a waste of your time—wrong attitude! You must change it. The subordinate is your mentee, your hire (read: your son or daughter).

Being a more successful leader is as easy as electing to spend a few extra minutes to focus on whomever we are talking to—to listen and work to understand what they're saying. Aren't those few extra minutes also a great investment in ourselves as well as our subordinates? What a win-win!

- Good leaders are good listeners. Effective leaders master the art of listening.
- Great leaders focus and work hard to really understand what the other person is saying—what they are really trying to communicate.
- We are in a leadership role whenever anyone reports to us, or simply wishes to share information or seek our advice.
- We can learn so much by really listening. Our silence can be golden.
- Shouldn't we treat our subordinate with at least as much respect as a good bottle of red wine? Good communication and effective leadership only require us to make the effort to open the speaker's water spigot all the way—and never impede the flow.

CHAPTER 2

LEADERSHIP—MISTAKE—A DIRTY WORD?

Mistakes are stepping-stones to success. Do not bury them in rationalization. Rationalizing them creates yet another link in the invisible chain that impedes our journey toward knowledge and enlightenment—it impedes our growth. Yet, too often, our first impulse is to justify our mistake by finding bases to support our decision, even though it wasn't the right one or, with hindsight and post-decision facts, not the best one. So, all too frequently, we accept our decision as good enough.

Good leaders make decisions. Great leaders correct poor decisions and/or adjust those that can be improved. Less effective or ineffective leaders wallow in the status quo of a rationalized unspoken mistake.

Let's analyze a recurring decision made by all leaders—hiring an employee. Let's assume your firm is hiring a receptionist. The receptionist is a key component of your company. She (or he) is the first impression of your organization on visitors and, more important, the first impression of your organization on every telephone caller.

Imagine a potential new client or customer calling your place of business. What impression will be developed if the telephone rings more than, say, three times? What if the caller has to wait for eight rings before the receptionist answers? What if there is no answer? What if the receptionist answers and immediately places the caller on hold? What if the caller asks to be connected to Mr. Jones and the receptionist simply responds that he is not in?

How would you like the receptionist to respond to each call? Wouldn't you prefer every call to be answered within three rings? Wouldn't you want the receptionist to offer to connect the caller to another person if Mr. Jones is unavailable, and then, if the answer is no, offer to take a message and give it to Mr. Jones, as well as invite the caller to leave a voicemail message?

How can you evaluate your hiring decision of the receptionist? You can wait for positive or negative feedback from your customers or clients, but chances are you will only hear the very best or very worst experiences, if that. Besides, what you really want to know is how your receptionist handles a typical call. Therefore, consider calling (anonymously) into your company's main switchboard number several times over, say, a three-month period.

In a sense, shouldn't we be confirming all of our decisions in this manner or in whatever follow-up is appropriate?

The elegance of the stock market is that we can make a decision every time we check the price of a stock. Once we check, we can immediately determine the success or failure of the decision. It doesn't matter if we are a trader or an investor. The cold hard current price, when compared to our purchase price, provides real-time feedback (read: from our customer or client). That feedback may prompt us to adjust our purchase decision in a variety of ways. We may elect to do nothing, and thereby make the decision to hold our stock position. We may elect to sell our position and recognize it was a mistake. Or, we may elect a variety of half-measures such as put or call options, or combinations thereof, to hedge our decision, thereby postponing the hard choice between hold and sell.

That stock market decision matrix, in principle, is no different from the matrix of decisions we make in a business context. The defining difference is that the stock market only involves money (or does it—doesn't it also involve our ego?), while most business decisions affect the lives of other people, sometimes those we know well and like.

Let's assume our anonymous calls to our office or company are answered, too often, after numerous rings. So we mention the delay to the newly hired receptionist. He advises that he is sometimes too busy to quickly respond to every call. What are our options? We can hire a second receptionist, we can purchase better equipment, we can offer more training, or we can replace the receptionist with someone we hope will be a more efficient operator.

Let's assume that not only are the calls answered slowly, but they are sometimes answered in a tone and manner that is not as friendly and helpful as we would like.

So, our stock seems to be going down. Do we hold or sell, or do we employ a hedging strategy by purchasing new equipment, an additional receptionist, or further training? In order to be able to make a decision to improve the situation, we must first be able to acknowledge (to ourselves) we made a mistake. Can we admit the mistake or will we do nothing and hope the receptionist's performance improves?

The applicable rule is simple. It states that, most of the time, what you see is what you get. So why then is this rule so often disregarded? It's because our ego does not allow us to acknowledge our mistakes, whether the purchase of a stock or the hiring of a receptionist. Our ego cannot tolerate the ignominy of failure which manifests itself by infusing within us a sense of weakness, even shame. Yet, our admission of failure, or a simple mistake, is a strength move. It is the strongest among us who acknowledge our foibles and failures. It is the weakest and most insecure among us who bury our foibles and failures and ignore or deny our mistakes.

Why is it that most of us disdain the thought of apologizing? Why is it that so many of us do not even recognize when an apology might be appropriate? It's the inability of our ego to even comprehend such an action. Our ego causes us to perceive an apology as failure, weakness and, perhaps, ineptitude. Our ego, when left completely unchecked, can even convince us that we are too important to *ever* have to apologize.

Were we to consider replacing the receptionist, our ego will try to stop us because it will perhaps not only seem callous to others, but will broadcast what may be perceived as a management failure for the whole office to see. Hence, our ego will convince us that we made the right hire, or a good enough hire, and that to acknowledge it was a mistake is only a sign of weakness.

So, we attempt to solve the receptionist problem by hoping a short, private comment about his slow response time will deliver the right message to catalyze the receptionist's self-improvement. But, as is usually the case, it works for a day or so, and thereafter the receptionist returns to his prior performance.

Perhaps you consider this scenario trivial. But it's not. How different is this decision matrix from dealing with an executive you hired who, for any number of reasons, is less effective than you would like? How different is this from dealing with a sales or marketing initiative you instituted that just isn't meeting your performance objectives?

Will your ego refuse to acknowledge the below-goal performance, or will you be able to recognize the problem and craft a solution? The elegance of the stock market is its constant evaluation of our investment or trading decisions. Will your ego allow you to accept that a loss on your investment was an investment mistake, or will it cause you to believe your investment decision was correct even though "the market disagrees" because the stock price keeps falling? Will you convert a failed short-term trade into a long-term investment by blaming the ineffectiveness of an anticipated near-term catalyst and then rationalizing a long-term outlook? Stock market treatises are replete with admonitions not to do so. Rather, they urge acceptance of the loss and moving forward.

Perhaps we are slow to fix a less-than-satisfactory decision because we invested so much time in the initial decision-making process. Why is it that most of us take too long to make a decision? Are we afraid of making a mistake, or perhaps compounding a mistake? Is such a scenario simply too much for our ego to take? The divorce courts are filled with parties who, when asked the question, often respond with the plaintive words, "I should have done this years ago, I knew it wasn't working and was a mistake. I don't know why I waited so long."

The answer, in part, is simply due to our desire to postpone the agony of dealing with a mistake or avoid the acknowledgement of failure by hoping things will improve. Of course, things almost never do. The law of inertia trumps good intentions. An object in motion stays in motion unless a countervailing force (read: curative action acknowledging error) is applied. You can check with Sir Isaac Newton if you don't believe me. There will be more to say about Sir Isaac in a later chapter.

Why do we so often perceive acknowledgement of a mistake as landing us a prominent place in the "Leadership Hall of Shame" when, in fact, it's the first step to a one-way ticket in the other direction. Why is it that one of the least-used phrases of leaders is "I apologize"? Why is it that most of us use it so rarely? It stands to reason that we can't fix our errors if we can't admit them to ourselves. Recognition is the springboard to remediation.

The admission of a mistake and, where appropriate, an apology is one of the universe's most effective cleansers (think of "Mr. Clean" being on your side!). Fixing a problem only wins the temporal battle. Acknowledging the mistake and apologizing if it hurt or negatively affected others wins the bigger battle—score a win for the power of grace and a loss for the forces of ego.

Great leadership requires frequent decision and re-evaluation followed by adjustment when necessary. Great leaders know when to soar like an eagle, but also when to glide back down to earth.

- Mistakes are not failures. Uncorrected mistakes are failures.
- Mistakes create learning experiences. Mistakes are the springboard for improvement.

- Don't let your ego bury your mistakes.
- "It's okay" or "it'll probably work out" thinking is a roadmap to mediocrity, or worse.
- Apologies are cathartic. If one is due, say it clearly to the person offended. Your karma will thank you.
- No matter how seemingly painful (to your ego), fix mistakes. The fix is a powerful cleanser on both the physical and spiritual planes.

CHAPTER 3

LEADERSHIP AND THE LAWS OF DELAY

Many of us take refuge in delay. But delay can be more often a house of pain than a safe-house. Effective leaders know every decision they make has an attendant cost. That cost may be hidden, not readily apparent, or immediately quantified. It's no wonder that great leaders think of delay as the decision to maintain the status quo. Effective leaders understand they are constantly evaluating the attendant cost-benefit matrix of status quo versus change.

The cost-benefit matrix analysis is obvious when, say, a leader considers whether or not to sell a new line of merchandise or create a new line of business. Of course, decisions are best made when all of the relevant facts are available and can be analyzed. But how often is that the case? Perhaps never. Why? Because business moves at an ever-increasing pace and new facts are constantly developing. Whether it's the emergence of a new competitor, the development of a more advanced product, or something else, the world of business constantly and rapidly evolves.

If we waited for all the available information—assuming it was obtainable—we could then make the "perfect decision." But perfection is illusory. That's why it's been said that perfection is the saboteur of completion. And that's why effective leaders are decision-makers, not perfectionists.

The quest for perfection creates delay. Delay represents the embrace of yesterday. It beckons us to look backward and live in the comfort of what is, and it prevents us from achieving what can be. Delay = Decisional Elongation Leaning Against Yesterday (D.E.L.A.Y.)!

Yet, delay can also be a powerful ally. Delay can be an effective strategy allowing leaders the opportunity to digest changes and create a window for further reflection, thereby allowing facts to continue to develop and be better understood. Effective leaders intuitively understand that delay is an effective tool when used thoughtfully, so long as it is not permitted to morph into procrastination and eventual paralysis.

Let's analyze an example of the positivity of delay used by effective leaders. Let's analyze our approach to a morning of e-mails. That initial barrage when we boot up our computer at the office or handheld device just after waking.

We gravitate to the headings that appear likely most important, and we open those messages first. We may delete e-mails with headings that suggest that they are either irrelevant or spam-like. We are prioritizing our review and response. But, the act of prioritizing is a form of delay. Electing to accelerate review of some e-mails and postponing the review of others allows us to use delay to be more effective.

That delay, however, is only effective to the extent we prioritize properly. When we postpone the review and/or response to an e-mail because we simply don't want to deal with its contents, our delay morphs into procrastination. Now, I'm not referring to an e-mail that requires our thought and analysis before we can properly and appropriately respond. I'm referring to those e-mails requiring a response which, for a variety of reasons, we elect to defer.

Ironically, effective leaders may intentionally elect to defer responding to an e-mail which seems to "beg" for a response. The sender may have e-mailed the leader seeking an answer to a question perhaps involving staffing or how to proceed on an issue when several options are available.

Effective leaders know when good leadership dictates a delayed response. How? Because the questions contained in some e-mails are best resolved by the sender. In fact, haven't we all responded to questions and issues after a delay only to learn that the sender resolved the issue? That scenario can bespeak effective leadership. Why? Because leaders know they enfeeble their subordinates if their subordinates fear making a decision on every issue without first checking with the boss. Effective leaders, therefore, know when to respond to these types of questions and furnish the answer or solution, but they also know when to give the subordinate more time to solve the situation on his or her own.

A well-known leader once told me he defers response to much of what crosses his desk, sometimes for several days. He added that more than half of the issues he deferred resolve themselves! By so doing, subordinates are allowed to make the decision. That leader well understood the need to support his subordinate's decision, even if not the best, and only suggested adjustment if truly necessary.

Let's analyze the impact of delay when it is clothed in apparent kindness. Let's analyze delay when it involves terminating an employee.

The termination of an employee is always tinged with the emotion of the confrontation and entwined with the recognition of failure.

Most of us dislike confrontation so, of course, we prefer to avoid it. But in the employment termination context, it is arguable that deferral is the crueler alternative. In fact, it usually is. Why?

It's cruel on two levels. It's cruel to the leader because the deferral protracts the agony, the dread of the confrontation. This self-inflicted cruelty, masked in the kindness we perceive we are exhibiting by postponing the pain, manifests itself in the leader in insidious ways. By dwelling on the confrontation, the leader feels the agony perhaps as a queasy stomach, some sleepless nights, or general anxiety spawned by indecision.

On the other hand, the cruelty inflicted upon the subordinate is even greater. Why? Because most of us know when we are underperforming or the job is just not working out. Sometimes, we feel it in the changed interactions with our peers. Sometimes, we feel isolation as others seek to avoid working with us, or simply avoid us.

I call this "death by a thousand pinpricks." Every day the underperforming employee comes to work he or she can sense the precarity of the situation. Perhaps the employee is receiving fewer assignments; perhaps the assignments have become less complicated, less important.

Eventually, other employees begin to resent the underperforming employee. He is not pulling his weight and others must pick up the slack. Not only do others have to work harder, they also know they can't rely on the weak employee and must further increase their workload by having to check the work of the weak employee.

Then, at some point, the weak employee starts to ask peers why he is getting less work or less complicated assignments. Usually, the response is a deflected answer. Either a half-truth, or a lie to lessen the pain, or avoidance via change of subject. Hence, a form of confrontation nevertheless develops among the affected employee and the other employees making all involved uneasy and creating a "dis-ease" in the workplace.

Effective leaders do not allow the "dis-ease" to develop or, if developed, to fester. They recognize the need for an immediate cure. Hence, while seemingly counterintuitive, the quicker the confrontation and implementation of a resolution, the better for all. Why? There are several reasons.

First, retaining an underperforming employee creates a double cost to the organization. Not only is the wrong employee on the job, but the right employee is prevented from filling the position until the wrong employee is removed, thereby exacerbating a deteriorating situation. Second, the underperforming employee is postponing the opportunity to find the right job that will allow his skills to shine. Many refer to their job as "the other wife" or "the other husband"; sometimes divorce is the solution, despite the attendant pain and disruption.

Accordingly, it should not be surprising that effective leaders terminate employees as soon as the need becomes clear. Less effective leaders delay the decision and hide behind rationales such as, "it's kinder to wait" or "perhaps the employee will yet turnaround."

However, turnarounds almost never occur in this context. In fact, effective leaders often know in the first few months if a hiring decision was optimal or nearly so. Why? Because almost always, what you see in the beginning is what you get. Reflecting on the marriage analogy, we know the divorce courts are filled with people who have said, "I thought I could change him or her."

But the maxim of that modern-day philosopher, Flip Wilson, usually prevails: "What you see *is* what you get."

So we can use delay to foster positive results, but never let delay devolve into procrastination. Once we recognize a decision matrix is upon us, whether we actively cause it or it is thrust upon us, effective leaders will make the decision. It may be right, wrong, or in that so-called grey area. Effective leaders know they will do the best they can. The very best leaders know decisions can be modified or overturned by simply making a follow-up decision. Avoiding the paralysis of delay begets the benefit of change. Life is change—or, perhaps change is life. Just compare the coral on the outer side of a coral reef, the side buffeted by the currents and tides of the not-so-pacific Pacific Ocean, to the calm lagoon-like inner side of the coral reef. The coral on the inner side, protected from the turbulence of the Pacific Ocean by the reef itself, is often a palette of pale florals (soft greens, pinks, etc.), a sort of "retirement community" of quiet and tranquility. On the other hand, the coral on the outer side of the coral reef is like Broadway, filled with rich, vibrant colors, full of life. They not only survive whatever the Pacific Ocean delivers. They thrive!

- Be a decision maker—don't try to be a perfectionist.
- Delays can be the device needed for further reflection or the development of new facts. Yet, extended and unnecessary delay—for example, delay due to the fear of decision—is corrosive.

- Unwarranted delay silently erodes the spirit—the spirit of the organization and all who are a part of it.
- Change, other than purely for the sake of change, is healthy.
- Effective leaders are the vibrant coral on the outer reef—the coral constantly buffeted by changing tides and currents as well as an occasional storm. Embrace change—nothing in our physical world remains constant.

CHAPTER 4
LOYALTY TO A FAULT

We all admire loyalty. Hollywood has glamorized loyalty so that it is virtually synonymous with courage and bravery. Perhaps you saw the stylized and less than historically accurate movie titled *The 300*. Against an overwhelming enemy, 300 Spartans sought to defend their beloved city-state knowing fully well they faced certain death at the hands of the mighty Xerxes, king of Persia. Yet, loyal to their warrior king, Leonidas, and to their country, they fearlessly defended Sparta, and were rewarded with a hero's death. This rear guard force of 300, despite impossible odds, was able to avoid being overrun for an extended period. While eventually annihilated by tens of thousands of Persian soldiers, the 300 provided the time and opportunity for the city-state to defend itself against a direct attack. The 300 held the enemy at bay, fighting on their terms from a strategic location.

We admire the loyalty, bravery, and courage of these fearless heroes just as we admire our armed service personnel as depicted in countless war movies (and real life) where the loyalty and bravery of a few save the many, or enable the many to live to fight yet another day.

Yet, just as loyalty can be virtually synonymous with courage and bravery, so, too, can it be a mask for fear and cowardice.

Loyalty can be defined as allegiance to one's country or sovereign, or one's devotion to a group or cause. Since this book is about leadership, let's focus on the second definition of loyalty: devotion to an organization, group, or cause.

It is in the business or commercial context that loyalty can be a two-edged sword. The ignoble aspects of loyalty manifest themselves when we hear or think phrases like, "Oh, he's just being loyal" or "Don't expect a straight answer from him, he's too loyal."

Effective leaders understand the two sides of loyalty and seek to develop the noble one. In the business context, it is not loyalty *per se* that is to be admired, but loyalty when properly directed.

In the business context, the sovereign is neither the leader nor anyone else in the organization. Similar to a city-state or a country, it is the organization itself. Employees, regardless of their position, owe their first loyalty to the company. They may admire and respect other employees. They may feel gratitude and/or fear toward the person who hired them, or to whom they report. They may feel beholden to those who help them more effectively perform their job and perhaps achieve higher status. However, their fundamental duty of loyalty must be to the entity itself. To be more loyal to an individual makes them, by definition, less loyal to the company. Of course, if the desires of their superior are completely in sync with the best interests of the organization, this convergence of loyalty is a manifestation of the effectiveness of the leader.

Yet, can any of us, even the greatest leaders, always seek initiatives and make decisions that can be said to be in the best interest of the company? Probably not. Even our greatest leaders are human. Therefore, even they are subject to human emotions that are sometimes strong enough to cloud their judgment.

Hence, subordinates loyal both to the company and their superior can sometimes be faced with the dilemma of divided loyalty. We call those employees who always support their boss, even when the decision may not be in the best interest of the entity, yes-men. A term that has developed a clear, pejorative connotation. So, it's no surprise that effective leaders seek to inculcate loyalty, but disdain yes-men. On the other hand, weak and ineffective leaders create an environment sufficiently comfortable for yes-men to survive and even prosper, although they silently disdain yes-men at the same time. Why?

On the one hand, leaders expect loyalty from their subordinates, especially when they are convinced their actions and decisions are in the best interest of the company. Therefore, they expect, even demand, unwavering allegiance to those decisions even if not to them. However, less effective leaders always expect primary loyalty to themselves, even when their decisions may be perceived by others as not the best courses of action for the company. But why do less effective leaders discourage loyalty to the company? Why do less effective leaders demand overarching loyalty to themselves?

Perhaps it's simply due to their ego. Perhaps the ego of less effective leaders cannot tolerate true dissent. Why not? Because their ego convinces them not only that their decisions are right and should not be questioned, but also that their subordinates are much less capable of making the best decision. Moreover, when the ego of the less effective leader mushrooms out of control, less effective leaders convince themselves of the "but for me" line of thinking. In other words, "But for me . . . you wouldn't have your job . . . you wouldn't have been promoted . . . the company would be less profitable . . . (fill in the blank)."

When an ineffective leader's ego is permitted to flourish, dissent is suppressed and blind adherence is at least expected and perhaps rewarded. Sometimes the reward manifests itself as a higher position or a salary increase. Oftentimes, when the less effective leader is questioned, it manifests itself as an insidious facial expression of disapproval, or if dissent is strenuously expressed, disdain.

So how can an effective leader encourage healthy dissent without fostering an environment of constant contradiction? It's easy. For one, at any meeting where a new initiative is being raised by the leader, no matter how clear the leader is in the direction to take, and no matter how passionate the leader is in his or her position, the effective leader opens the meeting to a full discussion and solicits all views. Rather than speak, effective leaders listen and work hard to facilitate a full and open dialogue. They accomplish their task by controlling their urge to respond to ideas they like or dislike. In fact, they respond either neutrally or positively to all suggestions. They ask question after probing question to elicit the entire thought process and basis for any attendee's comments and suggestions.

They know that effective questions, asked to reach the underlying basis for a comment, suggestion, or new idea, can be a compliment. They also know questions can be abusive either in content or tone. Hence, effective leaders work hard to ask questions in a neutral, inquisitive manner. They know that listening intently and asking follow-up questions, without ever cutting off the speaker, show respect for the speaker and her comments. As a result, attendees become more comfortable in the unfolding group dynamic and allow themselves to raise questions and ideas they might otherwise have felt embarrassed or fearful to discuss—fearful of being cut off, made fun of, or being the recipient of a laser-like look of scorn announcing to all in attendance that their comments were ill thought-through. Fear freezes comments and stifles ideas.

Effective leaders not only abjure yes-men, they seek to change them to thinking-men and why-men. How often do we say to another in an obviously disdainful manner, "Forget about what he thinks, he's too loyal"? But that's not what is really being said. What is really being said is either:

- he'll never raise a real issue; or
- he's "bought and paid for"; or

- he can't be trusted; or
- he's X's spy and lackey.

It all adds up to loyalty to a fault, blind loyalty to an individual rather than the company.

Why does an employee become more loyal to an individual as opposed to the company? Perhaps the employee knows or senses that a particular individual is his protector, someone who will protect him despite a bad decision or sub-par performance at his job. I'm not speaking about the classic "rabbi" or "priest" relationship. That is more in the nature of a positive mentor-mentee dynamic. All of us want a rabbi or priest as our boss to help us grow and achieve our goals. To the contrary, I'm talking about the type of misplaced loyalty that comes from either greed or fear that causes someone to be blindly loyal to another—the kind of loyalty that can actually sabotage a company.

Ah, so you think sabotage is too strong a word. Why? Sabotage is just as effective through silence, blind adherence, and inaction as by action. Sabotage can result from simply adding a component of critical mass (read: another "yes" vote) to support a less than effective idea or initiative. Support for a less-than-optimal idea can be just as damaging as placing a wooden shoe ("sabot") in the machinery of a better or more effective idea.

Yet, it goes against human nature to be the contrarian. When all of the attendees at a meeting are supporting an initiative, it's so much easier to go with the crowd. What if you are pondering a fact that wasn't fully discussed or not even raised, and which has negative implications. It's hard to raise the issue, isn't it? But that is the kind of loyalty (to the company) that reflects true courage!

Just think if you were the member of the famous Light Brigade of 600 who had the courage to suggest to your captain that he misunderstood his orders (not so easy in a military context, but not so hard in a corporate context—no employee has ever been court martialed!). What a hero you could have been!

This doleful stanza would then never have been written by Alfred, Lord Tennyson:

> "Some one had blunder'd:
> Their's not to make reply,
> Their's not to reason why,
> Their's but to do and die: . . ."

How sad that we mourn the loss of almost all of the 600 brigadiers because no one dared mention the blunder. In the corporate context, you might say a blunder just costs money, not lives; but it isn't just money. When costly mistakes are made and business deteriorates, often staff are fired. It may not be life and death to the surviving employees, but it will surely feel that way to some who were terminated.

Be loyal to all you hold dear, most importantly your integrity and character. Don't lose sight of the hierarchy of priorities. Sycophantism by any name is quicksand for our character. Don't misplace loyalty. The longer it remains misplaced, the harder it is to find. Your karma will thank you, and so will your self-esteem.

- Seek loyalty—abjure loyalty to a fault.
- Effective leaders seek "input-men," not yes-men.
- Effective leaders drill through the "desire to go with the crowd response"—they seek independent, thoughtful opinion.
- Ineffective leaders seek rubber stamp associates. Weak leaders demand blind obedience.
- Yes-men are organizational phantoms—they lack presence on any level.

CHAPTER 5

EFFECTIVE LEADERSHIP THROUGH THE EYES OF SIR ISAAC NEWTON

When Sir Isaac Newton wrote his seventeenth century work on the laws of motion (*Philosophiæ Naturalis Principia Mathematica*, July 5, 1687), he was most likely thinking about classical mechanics, not leadership. Yet, much of his genius is employed by effective leaders who recognize that the "body" to which Newton refers could be the corporate or organizational body or the body politic.

Leaders of companies are responsible for the growth of their companies. For leaders of virtually any firm that means (to paraphrase Peter Drucker) attracting more clients and customers and keeping them, while at the same time continuing to attract new ones.

To grow the health and profit of any organization, leaders must continuously evaluate the firm's velocity and direction, bringing us to Newton's First Law. To paraphrase, companies at rest tend to stay at rest. If the company is not growing, the question becomes, "Why is it not growing and what measures should be taken to facilitate growth?" Of course, what we are really talking about is the ability to embrace change—the change necessary to create new growth and the change necessary to constantly strive to optimize a current growth trajectory.

Yet change is challenged by Newton's First Law, which postulates the persistence for bodies at rest to remain so. Moreover, Newton's First Law of "status quo" may be seen to be further supported by Newton's Third Law. To paraphrase and adapt to this context, every action to create change is met with an equal and opposite reaction to maintain stasis, or the status quo.

Hence, leaders have to work extra hard to effect change. Good leaders know change is healthy. Great leaders know change is healthy and errors are far from disastrous, they are merely rungs on the learning curve ladder enabling leaders to adjust and constantly improve their initiatives. Their ego neutralized, effective leaders can tolerate, even embrace, dissent and human impediments. They absorb the antithesis of detractors to continually improve the synthesis of ideas and improve initiatives. The German philosopher, Georg W.F. Hegel, was dialectically clear about that equation: thesis plus antithesis yields synthesis.

By neutralizing the fears and insecurities which could allow the ego of leaders to disregard the ideas of others (whether in the form of complaint or different approach or even outright disagreement), effective leaders can embrace pushback and adjust their initiatives to reflect useful feedback from others.

Effective leaders know that business as usual is a recipe for stunted, or worse, negative growth. Whether called the "new normal" or the "new paradigm," business is changing at a constantly faster rate (*i.e.,* the so-called second derivative, which is the rate of change *of* the rate of change). We need only consider the increasing speed at which new devices are developed to enable us to more effectively and productively use the Internet and broadband in order to understand the accelerating rate of change that constantly bombards us.

Yet, human nature seems to pull us back to bask in the known and to fear the unknown. Ironically, it is only after change is implemented that the "body-corporate" slowly begins to fully embrace its benefits and recognize its beneficial impact on the organization.

Let's analyze the changes occurring in the delivery of legal services. In the past, the accepted norm was ever-increasing hourly rates and, therefore, ever-increasing legal budgets. However, starting at about the middle of the first decade of the twenty-first century, in-house counsel was mandated to effect change (*i.e.,* reduce legal costs), and if working for a public company, was being challenged to continue to do so on an annual, if not quarterly, basis. Outside lawyers may allow themselves to believe this initiative will be temporary, to end when the economy recovers. They are probably wrong. The cost-cutting directive being applied by corporate America is likely to become the "forever" normal, and, therefore, the application of the rubber band theory (or the "return to the mean" theory), which suggests most things snap back to where they were or to their mean, may well remain elusive.

For inside counsel to understand how best to execute the cost-cutting directive emanating from the financial department, and, on the other hand, for outside counsel to understand how to grow profitably in this belt-tightening environment, inside and outside counsel must analyze the constituent legal services being sought or offered, respectively, by placing them in one of two buckets (let's keep it simple).

Let's call the first bucket those services perceived to be "widget-like," or commodity services, and let's call the second bucket those services perceived to be enhanced-value services.

Outside counsel may allow themselves to be offended by terms such as widget and commodity. It's perfectly understandable. Isn't the law a noble profession? Isn't what most lawyers do for a living more or less noble? Of course it is, but the change that has occurred and must be accepted by outside counsel is the bifurcation of professional services, which seems to create a distinction between the nobility of defending the Constitution and our human rights, and the business of commercial law which (less nobly) merely facilitates a transaction or is applied to litigate a commercial dispute. There will be much more on litigation in the final chapters of this book since many of us are, at least some of the time, either buyers or sellers of litigation services.

Once outside counsel accepts the differentiation, it is necessary to analyze those elements of its commercial practice to determine which are commoditizing and which are value-enhancing.

Let's compare a law firm to a simplified model of an accounting firm as a basis for analysis in order to create a going-forward strategy.

Let's assume the accounting firm only has two departments, a tax department and an audit department. Let's further assume the tax department furnishes value-enhanced advice (everyone wants to save on taxes), and the audit department is furnishing a commoditized service (auditing the books and preparing tax returns) that clients can purchase from any accounting firm. Let's further assume the tax code is incredibly complex and clients need top tax advice to create lower tax rate long-term capital gain ("LTCG") as opposed to higher tax rate ordinary gain ("OG"). Let's further assume federal income tax rates on OG have a top bracket of 70% and LTCG gains are taxed at 20%. Clearly, in this scenario, the tax department offers enhanced value if their members are expert at increasing LTCG and reducing OG. As a result, clients seek to use the firm's tax department and are willing to use the firm's audit department (even if their rates seem pricey).

Now, let's assume the world changes and the rate for OG is reduced to, say, 36% and LTCG rate remains at, say, 20%. Let's further assume the tax code is simplified to reduce or eliminate many of the sophisticated techniques that were used to convert OG to LTCG and create the concomitant substantial tax savings for clients.

Under this change of circumstances (read: too many lawyers able to furnish basic litigation and basic transactional services, or too many supermarkets in a given area, etc.), how is our accounting firm now positioned with its two-department model? While nothing has changed to affect the audit department, the "value" of the tax department has been diminished by virtue of the decrease in the marginal highest tax rate for OG, and the removal of sophisticated cost savings techniques from the Internal Revenue Code used by top flight tax accountants to create LTCG or convert OG to LTCG. As a result, without the enhanced value of the tax department being able to drive clients to the firm, the audit department becomes the main driver of business.

Yet, the audit department is not an enhanced-value service as was the tax department. As a result, clients are no longer willing to pay pricey audit fees in order to enjoy the enhanced value of the firm's tax department. Without a special reason to use the firm's audit department, clients now seek to lower their audit expenses. Why? Because, on a standalone basis, the audit department appears to offer no enhanced value and begins to be perceived solely as a commodity (whether that perception is correct is irrelevant; all that is relevant is the reality of the perception). Hence, price begins to become an issue, as it invariably does in connection with all sales of commodities. Once price becomes an issue, price compression ensues and spreads to the audit departments of most accounting firms if their audit department is an important component of their business. The situation, of course, must be reversed by creating another value-enhanced service to drive clients to the firm on an "enhanced skill-based" versus a "cost-based" platform or by converting the audit department, at least in part, to an enhanced-value service.

This painful analogy may well apply to any organization, and certainly to law firms. For a law firm that provides, say, mortgage and house closings, without more, their business is being commoditized (and exacerbated by the woefully weak housing sector) requiring consideration of a low-cost model approach. Perhaps they will become subject to a "zero sum game" (*i.e.,* a fancy phrase for continuously lower prices), if the work can be outsourced, in whole or in part, to lawyers in India or China (working with a domestic local title company), or to the in-house or outside lawyer recently terminated and working at reduced rates on a per transaction basis from his home. It's tough for any law firm to compete with the overhead model of a home-office lawyer when the services competed for can be single-lawyer outsourced and are considered basic or commoditized.

As a general principle, there is little doubt that the new normal of a constantly cost-cutting model is here to stay, at least until, if ever, the immutable laws of supply and demand cause a rebalancing of the leverage between the purchaser and provider of legal services. Perhaps a rebalancing will occur when aspiring lawyers eschew law school for other pursuits.

What must a leader consider to keep the law firm profitable and growing? For one, consider discontinuing or reducing services that compete with lawyers in India, and the lawyers in China who will surely follow the Indian model and become fluent in English. Second, consider discontinuing or reducing work that can be effectively replicated by a solo practitioner working from home. In other words, either jettison the commodity-type work, or develop a platform that allows for delivery of that work on a cost-effective basis without an unacceptable drop in quality. Of course, that may require a new platform for delivery of these legal services in order to maintain some level of profitability (perhaps a two-tiered associate program with certain associates being paid lower salaries commensurate with the lower hourly rate for the work they are performing; and/or, perhaps, a new compensation system based on deals closed, a so-called "piece-work" system). In either case, quality control will be required.

I said unacceptable drop when referring to quality because lawyers know that it is not necessary to achieve a "100" on every project (unless perhaps the client is your mother!). In fact, in-house counsel understand that the law of diminishing returns applies to legal work. In-house counsel understand that most projects can be well satisfied with a grade of 90 to 95. Scant few legal assignments require a perfect score and scant few should ever be worked to achieve a perfect score. Why? Because the effort required to bring a project, say a research assignment, from a grade of 95 to 100, may require almost double the amount of hours! Hence, part of the new normal for leaders of law firms is to manage their staff more effectively.

Review and control is anathema to practitioners of the noble profession. However, leaders of commercial law firms understand its necessity because the era of "get it perfect regardless of cost" has disappeared, unless the matter rises to a bet-the-ranch level.

As shown in our law firm example, effective leaders of any organization must constantly determine which of the services they provide fall within (or will in the future fall within) the commodity bucket, and which services fall within, (or can be made in the future to fall within) the enhanced-value bucket.

This analysis is an introspection which is bound to require "pain relievers" (what I call the Aspirin Analysis) until solutions are found. All of this will result in change. To many practitioners, the legal profession seemed static—it never was.

What solutions can the law firm leader, or any leader, initiate to ameliorate the inevitable call from in-house counsel or an important customer indicating that fees or prices not only cannot increase, but for commodity-type work must be reduced?

First, the leader must help the firm to grapple with this fundamental change that law firms must undergo in their culture in order to survive and prosper. A cultural shift from the furnishing of legal services to that of a vendor's services, at least with respect to the commoditizing and commoditized elements of the services, must be recognized. This recognition and acceptance is essential if law firms wish to survive and prosper. And, it applies to every organization.

Effective leaders understand there will be pushback. But they also know that those who embrace and adjust to the change will emerge stronger and healthier. They know a positive outcome will emerge because nature teaches us that creatures who survive a hardy life are more vibrant and robust than those enjoying a placid life. Remember the coral beds on the ocean side of a barrier reef where the waves and currents constantly buffet the coral versus the coral beds on the tranquil lagoon side. Pick it! Either the lagoon side which is pale and pastel coral, or the ocean-side coral with its kaleidoscope of rich, strong, vibrant colors. Which will you choose?

Effective leaders know they must select the outer side of the reef to survive and prosper in the "new normal." Why? Because if we were living coral and had the option to live quietly on the protected lagoon side of the reef as opposed to the rough outer side where storms, winds and currents are virtually our daily lot, we might naturally select the tranquil side (read: status quo).

Which brings us to Newton's Second Law: F=ma. The "F" in "F=ma" is the measure of the force of a leader to effect change. But force is seldom, if ever, a good motivator for lawyers or accountants or, for that matter, any employee. Lawyers are best led by an effort to help them to see (and accept by themselves) the benefit of change, rather than by edict. Why? Because most lawyers are over-achievers they seek, above all, respect for their intelligence. Moreover, law firm leaders know they must work hard to help them overcome their innate (and sometimes overwhelming) aversion to risk. Is it really any different for any employee of any organization? Aren't lawyers just like the rest of us? Few prefer being told what to do instead of realizing it for themselves (with or without guidance). Effective parents realize this. Is the corporate leadership role that much different?

The "m" in "F=ma" is the mass of the effort of the leader to create change. It is the number of initiatives and approaches used by the leader to educate the members of the organization to the need for change and adoption of new paths. Last, the "a" in "F=ma" is the intensity applied by the leader. Newton calls it acceleration, but speed and intensity are, in a sense, synonymous, since the greater the speed the lesser the gaps in between the applications to effect the initiative. Hence, the greater intensity.

Resistance to change is resistance to growth—and, for some, is the equivalent of resistance to life itself. Resistance to growth may be seen as tantamount to the acceptance of erosion and decline.

It is virtually axiomatic that nothing at rest actually stays at rest. Why? Because we do not live in a vacuum or in a world of zero net force, a static world. Newton taught us that his First Law only applies if there are no other forces at work (*i.e.*, zero net force). But effective leaders well know there are always forces at work; they may just be imperceptible at the moment. Great leaders constantly seek to perceive the imperceptible. They seek to divine the next competitor, the next direction, the next initiative, the next game-changer.

Great leaders constantly work to understand emerging trends. They know a new trend is like a train leaving the station. As it leaves the platform it is moving slowly enough to easily jump on board. However, once the train pulls out, jumping on board becomes dangerous or impossible. Jumping on board may be jarring, but when effectively done, allows the "business athlete" to move ahead of the competition, perhaps even, with a nod to Newton and his successors, move a quantum leap ahead.

- Inertia is an insidious saboteur.
- The forces of the status quo press against us like the invisible pressure of air. This unseen resistance makes it harder to move forward and grow. But far from impossible.
- Effective leaders seek to change the status quo—they prod and press because they know the danger of staying in a comfort zone too long.
- New initiatives, new ideas are the lifeblood of any organization.

- Even a time-tested successful old product can always be produced more efficiently, somehow made even better or simply marketed better.
- Remember TaB, Coke's zero calorie diet cola product introduced in the sixties. Then New Coke was introduced—a flop. Then, voila, we have Coke Zero. It may not be correlative, but as of this writing, Coke seems to be beating Pepsi in the "cola wars."

Chapter 6

LEADERSHIP—AND THE "EXTRA MILE"

Effective leaders understand the negativity of the phrase "go the extra mile." They know success usually only requires going an extra foot. Sometimes, it's just going an extra few inches.

In the 2010 "fastest man in the world" event, the indoor 60-meter dash, Dwain Chambers won the world title. Mr. Chambers bested a world-class field of seven by sprinting 60 meters in 6.48 seconds. The last place finisher ran the same distance in 6.72 seconds. How interesting that a mere 24 hundredths of a second separated stardom from relative obscurity. How interesting that an approximately 4% time spread differentiated the race's best runner from the race's worst runner.

Effective leaders understand that the 60-meter dash is a metaphor for success in most aspects of life. Success seldom requires going the extra mile. Often, just 5% or 10% more effort is all it takes to make a difference. Vice President Al Gore knows this all too well. After his failed presidential bid in 2004, Mr. Gore learned firsthand that success and failure can differentiate themselves by only the slightest of margins (and in his case, some important judicial decisions which would not have required adjudication had the voting differential been, perhaps, just ½ of 1% greater).

Effective leaders inculcate in others a desire to succeed. They understand that motivation is a critical aspect of their job. Therefore, they seek to foster in others a desire to do their best. In that vein, the phrase "go the extra mile" becomes a healthy leadership technique. In fact, perhaps even graceful. Why? In ancient times, Roman law allowed a Roman soldier to require a civilian to carry his backpack for a mile. It was, however, only a Roman mile. A Roman mile approximated 1000 paces or about 1.48 kilometers. All but a few might have enjoyed the requirement, although it is reasonable to assume that most resented it. But teachings of the time, as embodied in the New Testament, urged civilians to do even more: If the requirement was one mile, carry the burden for two miles. Hence, the phrase "go the extra mile." Perhaps this expression is really asking us to extend ourselves—physically, mentally, or emotionally—and thereby extend and enhance our inner grace.

Of course, the challenge for corporate leaders is to instill both a sense of self-worth and dedication in an effort to motivate each member of the team to give the project the extra effort. Ironically, success often requires much less than going the extra mile. Usually, just another 5% or 10%.

Why is it that the difference between mediocrity and success can turn on such a razor-thin margin? How can it be that a mere 5% or 10% additional effort can make such a difference? Often it makes the difference between a grade of A and a grade of B (or the difference between first and last place in a 60-meter dash), whether the grade is on an exam in high school or college, or in the exam of life.

Let's consider a scenario in which many of us have found ourselves. Perhaps it was a demonstration we had been asked to make in our science class in high school on a particular chemical reaction, a presentation in our English class about an author whose work we were studying, or perhaps we have been asked to make a presentation to our colleagues on a particular issue or concept. Each task is essentially the same. All the students in the science class were studying the chemical reaction. All the students in the English class were reading the same works of the author being studied. And all of your colleagues have a working knowledge of the issue or concept about which you've been asked to speak.

In each instance, we can assume the audience to whom we are speaking has studied, or is as familiar with, the topic—at about the same level as we were—when we were first tapped to give our presentation to our colleagues. We can also assume each attendee will continue to study and become more conversant with the topic, basically at the same pace as before. Why should they do more? They are not the person giving the presentation. You are.

Regardless of the milieu, school or work, you want to know at least as much about the topic as the other attendees, and preferably more. Why? It just makes sense that, on the one hand, you don't want any attendee to embarrass you and, on the other hand, you would like to impress your boss and your colleagues. You know everyone will be studying, and/or thinking about your presentation. Let's assume the presentation will take place in 10 business or school days (we'll give everyone the weekend off), and that each attendee puts in an hour every other day studying or thinking about the topic. Hence, each attendee invests 5 hours, in total, in preparation for your presentation. Of course, they are not specially preparing. All they are doing is either their normal study routine or work routine, but it is nevertheless a passive form of preparation. You, however, need to actively prepare.

Knowing you have 10 business days, plus the interim weekend, let's say you decide to use every day to prepare for ½ hour each day, a total of 6 hours of preparation (versus 5 for the attendees). Your preparation time will exceed each attendee's by 1 hour, a 20% increase over the effort of each attendee. But, you want to shine during the presentation so you go the extra mile and prepare for an additional 2 hours, thereby tripling your extra-mile effort. To do so, you only needed to add 10 minutes a day (beyond the 30 minutes you already planned to spend) over the 12-day period to give you a 60% (3 hour) versus only a 20% (1 hour) preparation time advantage over the attendees. How did you do it? Perhaps you crammed the entire extra 2 hours the night before the presentation. It really doesn't matter. The mathematics is indisputable. By adding an average of 10 minutes per day to your daily preparation routine, or one-third more effort (over the 30 minutes per day you might have otherwise done), you increased your expertise level from 20% (6 hours versus 5 hours) to 60% (8 hours versus 5 hours). Hence, a one-third increase in daily effort (a mere 10 minutes), in this case, produced the opportunity to create a knowledge premium of 60% versus 20% or a 200% increase in extra-mile premium.

The key is the delta. The delta represents the measure of the difference between two numbers. Hence, if one student scores a 90 on an exam and another scores an 80, the delta is 10. Whenever we make comparisons, it's always about the delta. The delta reflects the differential. In this case, the calculation is the differential in preparation time which, in this instance, we are equating to a knowledge differential.

As we learned from the runner who finished last to Dwain Chambers in the 60-meter dash, when compared to others, it's not what you know or how fast you are. Rather, it's about how much more you know or how much faster you are (relative to the others).

Effective leaders well understand the delta concept. They know absolutes may have worked for Lord Kelvin (who "discovered" absolute zero kelvin), but outside the laboratory, in the cauldron of real life, those who reach 212° Fahrenheit bubble up to the top while the others at, say, 200° Fahrenheit, just float along with the masses. Imagine you at 212° enjoying the bubbly delight of victory while your competitor languishes at 211° in defeat or, at best, second place.

The point is elegant. Effective leaders know they don't need a team of Stephen Hawkings to run a successful organization. They know that Dr. Hawking's knowledge of quantum mechanics was perhaps only 10%

greater than his peers in the field of physics. That 10% delta, however, made him a leader in his field. Dr. Hawking may be a genius to us, but in a field of geniuses he only needs to be 10% more of a genius, maybe less. Similarly, effective leaders understand the application of this principle to every day corporate life. It's the principle of "relative expertism" (or, if you prefer, relative expertise).

They know that, if most have a knowledge level of, say, 7 on a scale of 10, the person whose level is at 8, or even just 7½, is the expert. They know that a mere 14.28% more expertise (1/7th), even half of that, can qualify an individual as an expert, at least relatively. And, as Einstein famously pointed out, everything is relative! Hence, effective leaders don't motivate for perfection, they motivate (others) to achieve relative expertism. Effective leaders know that perfection is the saboteur of success. Imagine the team of a truly effective leader, each member a relative expert in his or her sphere of responsibility. Isn't that exactly the team an effective leader strives to assemble? Of course it is!

Effective leaders know that all of their subordinates can be successful and achieve inner fulfillment from doing so. Success is measured in countless ways, oftentimes as basic as just getting over the finish line, regardless of how long it takes. Just speak to some of those who finished at or near last place in the New York City or Boston marathons. Don't you consider the wheelchair or otherwise handicapped contestant who finished the race just as much a winner as anyone or everyone else, even if they finished last or near to last?

Effective leaders instill subordinates with the yearning for success and find countless ways to help them to achieve it. They may not know if it will take an extra mile (or if you are a Roman, 1.48 kilometers) to achieve success, but they absolutely know that the smallest successes breed more of the same.

- Effective leaders are motivators.
- Effective leaders know that sometimes only a razor-thin margin separates the good job done from the great job done.
- Hence, effective leaders seek to instill an extra effort ethic.
- Extra effort comes in many shapes and forms. Sometimes nothing more than re-checking a series of calculations. Sometimes the complete rewrite of a report because the first draft was based on an incorrect premise.

- As my father taught me at a very young age, "good, better, best . . . never let it rest . . . until the good is better and the better (your) best." My father never sought perfection, but he always did his best. He was never afraid to invest the extra effort. Thanks for the lesson, Dad.

CHAPTER 7

LEADERSHIP AND MOTIVATION

If we break down leadership into its core components, we might determine the primary components to be:

- Motivating others individually and collectively to harness their ability to enhance their self-worth and self-esteem; and
- Motivating others to enhance their worth to the organization.

What are the motivational aspects of leadership and the techniques to motivate others? More important, how can they become self-reinforcing? How does a leader create the necessary stimuli to make motivation self-perpetuating?

If we think of motivation as a rocket ship within each of us, the obstacles to success become obvious. If we wish the rocket ship to ascend beyond the Earth's gravitational pull, which constantly tries to draw us back (to crash and burn), we begin to recognize and accept the need for booster rockets—the required additional thrust (read: necessary motivation) beyond the rocket's initial liftoff. With sufficient bursts of additional thrust, we can eventually reach outer space. Once there, we are, at that moment, traveling beyond gravitational pull. In other words, we will continue to move forward and only fall back or fall down if the gravitational pull of another body draws us in and down. Unlike spaceships, we become susceptible to falling back or down when we let ourselves get down, usually as a result of the effect of another body, however, a human, not a celestial one. Perhaps an uninspiring and negative boss, an angry spouse, or a jealous colleague whose negativity we allow to seep inside, infecting us with thoughts of failure and rejection. Perhaps a setback due to a change in circumstances over which we had no control.

On the one hand, how do we find our booster rockets? How do we overcome flashes of negativity? That's done with self-motivation, belief in ourselves, and recognition that failure and rejection are to be absorbed as learning experiences, not barricades, fences, or black holes. On the other hand, if we are to be effective leaders, if we are the mentor, how do we furnish the fuel to ignite the booster rockets within our reports, subordinates, and peers? Effective leaders mentor, in a sense, everyone within their organization. However, the mentoring effort may vary from an almost non-measurable indirect effort to a material one-on-one effort. Effective leaders understand their supports so they know, often intuitively, when and whom to motivate.

However, just as leaders must mentor others (or identify mentors for others), they know it is critical for them to find their own mentors. The most effective leaders recognize that the advice and counsel of a trusted mentor can turn their good ideas into great ideas by mixing another's thoughts and wisdom with them. Yet, many leaders not only do not have mentors, they refuse to either seek them out or recognize them despite their presence, availability, and willingness, even though mentors exist everywhere.

Why can't less effective leaders find mentors? Why can't they even see them? Their ego blinds them. Their ego enflames their fears and distorts the recognition of the benefit of a mentor by blinding them with an opaque veil of weakness, insecurity, and foolish overconfidence.

The term "mentor" derives from a relationship written about by Homer in his classic work about Greek mythology, *The Odyssey*. Mentor seems to have been both male and female, or at least to have had certain characteristics of each. Before he left to fight the Trojan War on the side of Athens, Odysseus asked his trusted friend Mentor, a male, to look after his son, Telemachus. Later on, the goddess Athena had disguised herself as Mentor, and it was she who provided the courage and wisdom to Telemachus, enabling him to speak to a king (read: boss or superior) and earn his respect. As a result, Telemachus becomes history's first famous mentee.

Homer's Mentor was a person who offered protection and also tutelage, guidance, perhaps even nurturing. Perhaps, as a result of François Fénelon's work *Les Aventures de Télémaque*, the modern word for mentee, "protégé," which is the French equivalent of "the protected or looked-after," came into common usage.

Regardless of which word we use, mentee, protégé, or even Telemachus, Webster's definition is clear and precise: a person guided or helped in the furtherance of his or her career by another more influential person. Similarly, mentor is equally succinctly defined: advisor, loyal friend, teacher, or coach.

The beauty of a mentor-mentee relationship is the benefit to both mentor and mentee, no doubt more often than not equally rewarding. Just consider the facial expressions of Pat Morita, who played the character of the mentor in *The Karate Kid* (the original or any of the sequels). Pat Morita's character, Mr. Miyagi, expresses a variety of emotions throughout the movie, but the transcending and most moving expression is satisfaction and fulfillment as he watches his student battle through pain and setback to grow as a martial arts expert and, more important, evolve as a young man. On the other hand, consider the facial expressions of Ralph Macchio, who played the character of the mentee in *The Karate Kid.* Perhaps the signature expression surfaced on the karate kid when he overcame his fears, succeeded in the martial arts championship tournament, succeeded for his mentor, and, most important, succeeded for himself. Perhaps you haven't seen the movie. It's a heartwarming story of a boy who moves from Newark, New Jersey to Los Angeles' San Fernando Valley, where he is bullied by a vicious group of kids learning karate and being taught by a "take-no-prisoners" sensei. Perhaps most appealing about the original 1984 box office hit is the evolution of the mentor-mentee relationship between the karate kid and his mentor. At first, Ralph is overcome with awe; however, the relationship eventually morphs into one of surrogate father-son. Eventually, mutual respect and admiration. The performance of the mentor, Pat Morita, was strong enough to earn him a nomination for an Academy Award for best supporting actor. How fitting for the role of a mentor and motivator to be nominated for an Academy Award as a support system. Of course, many movies are filled with mentor-mentee relationships. But, what counts in these relationships is the classic evolution of the mentee from a student, filled with self-doubt, seeking to excel solely to please his teacher (or perhaps, in part, in fear of his teacher), to a more mature version of himself filled with inner security respectful of his mentor and, therefore, respectful of himself.

What Homer doesn't tell us, however, is exactly how Mentor earns the trust of Telemachus. Perhaps Telemachus simply accepted his father's selection of Mentor as his protector and counselor. Perhaps Telemachus was beguiled by Athena when she was disguised as Mentor. Beguiled by her beauty, no doubt, but most likely also her sincerity, friendship, and motherly love.

Effective leaders are not gods or demi-gods (although perhaps the ineffective ones think of themselves that way). They must work hard to motivate others and earn their trust. They must put aside their fear of being dethroned someday by those they train and support. To the contrary, effective leaders seek to mentor all those who may be capable of being their successor. Effective leaders must work hard to find ways to help their subordinates help themselves. They know that handouts do not work. Just as President Franklin Delano Roosevelt's "Good Neighbor" policy failed to work on its South American beneficiaries, either economically or politically, so, too, are handouts often paid back with a "bite to the hand that fed them."

Effective leaders also know that motivation is always subject to being eroded, even destroyed. Effective leaders understand that the force of gravity from the fear of failure is always trying to pull down motivation. Oftentimes, it surfaces in unseen and insidious ways not discernible to the subordinate, much less to his or her senior—perhaps jibes from a "friendly" overly competitive colleague.

Motivation, just like a rocket ship, can be pulled down whenever it gets too close to the negative pull of a foreign or unfriendly body, or agonizing circumstance. Effective leaders understand how easy it is to maintain a high motivational level when "all systems are go" and everything is on course. Similarly, they know that the true challenge is to maintain a strong motivational level or prevent erosion when the motivational ship is starting to veer off course. Perhaps a subordinate is coping with a school problem with a child, a marital issue, or a health problem. Effective leaders are always on the lookout for warning signs. Red flags are red flags regardless of size, and a warning sign is a warning sign regardless of the way in which it manifests itself.

Effective leaders understand, just like doctors, that problems are often lurking when there are changes. When it comes to health issues, changes are often warning signs. That's why doctors always ask, at some point during the office visit, "Is anything different, has anything changed?" Doctors know changes need to be investigated. Likewise, effective leaders can always sense changes in behavior. Why? Because they pay attention to the little things as well as the big ones. They focus and they listen with their ears, eyes, and heart. That way they can see, or hear, the little things, the little changes. They know most of us can hide the big changes, and that it's the little changes that offer the "tell." We are all pretty good at covering up our problems, but no one is good enough to cover all of them up all of the time. Perhaps President Abraham Lincoln said it best. To paraphrase and stretch a quote: "You can fool effective leaders some of the time, and average leaders all of the time, but you can't fool effective leaders all of the time."

In other words, half the battle of being a good motivator and an effective leader is knowing when to apply a rocket boost, some extra motivation. Effective leaders are able to determine when to allow the rocket ship to gracefully travel through outer space on its own, and when to exercise a little thrust in order to effect the slight course changes that may avert a crash or simply keep the rocket ship on course.

Effective leaders understand that motivation can be instilled in others by imparting a belief in the other's ability to succeed, by enhancing their self-esteem. Can it be that easy? Yes! Years ago a study was conducted among a group of students at an elementary school. Two sections were created. Section A was labeled the advanced section, and Section B was labeled the average section.

The students involved in the study were told that the better ones would be placed in the advanced section, Section A, while the other students would be placed in the average section, Section B. The students were then told (misinformed) they would be selected for each section based on their ability to succeed after analyzing each student's intelligence test scores and past performance. However, in fact, each student was selected at random. No selection was based on relative merit. Each student was blindly placed in a section. As a result, both sections were filled with a mixture of superior and average students. Once the sections were created, the students selected for Section A were told they were all the best students and expected to excel. On the other hand, the students selected for Section B were told that they were not the better students and that only average performance was expected of them.

The results of the study were fascinating. Every one of the students in Section A excelled, including the average students randomly placed there. On the other hand, the students in Section B performed at a level below that of the Section A students, even though the number of above-average students was approximately equal in both sections.

Each section had a similar amount of superior and average students. So what caused the superior performance of the students placed in Section A, even though the section was composed of both superior and average students?

The answer seems to be the effect of motivation. In this study, the Section A students were told they were "A-type" students and they were expected to excel. In fact, they did, whether they were above-average or average students. On the other hand, the students of Section B were told they were "average students" and expected to perform at just an average level. In fact, they did perform at an average level, whether they were above-average or average students.

Motivation is a powerful elixir. By raising expectations and imparting a belief that higher goals can be achieved, higher goals become achievable. And, higher goals are then often achieved. Similarly, "negative motivation" can limit performance to an average level even by those capable of performing at a higher level.

By virtue of Mr. Miyagi imparting his belief in Ralph (the karate kid) that he could achieve mastery of his martial arts studies, Ralph began to believe in himself. Mr. Miyagi's motivational thrusts propelled Ralph to higher levels of achievement and success. Effective leaders know that these same principles work equally well in the workplace.

Effective leaders understand that their efforts to motivate others are intended to start or accelerate motion to achieve, excel, or just successfully finish a project. Effective leaders well understand the Newtonian principle of inertia. Hence, they seek to embrace its positivity by creating, maintaining, or accelerating the motion of others. There's plenty of time for a body at rest to stay at rest, in this lifetime or otherwise.

- Motivation is fragile. We must constantly work to overcome the trespasses and other impediments which can erode our motivation.
- Successful motivation is a function of instilling self confidence and self-esteem. We should always work to neutralize our ego which beckons us to wallow in self pity and retaliatory thoughts.
- Effective leaders understand that motivation requires nurturing—self nurturing or nurturing by a mentor.
- The best leaders understand their need to maintain a high personal level of motivation.
- Even the most highly motivated from time to time need a booster shot of mentoring, whether from a colleague, friend, or trusted advisor.
- The best leaders understand they, too, need mentors.

CHAPTER 8

LEADERSHIP AND THE SPEED OF LIGHT

Light travels at the speed of 186,000 miles per second. Nothing in our universe travels anywhere near that fast, or if something does, we have yet to discover it. Yet, sometimes we feel as if things seem to move that fast. Effective leaders well understand that a frenetic pace, a pace at which we strive to constantly move faster, often can cause a variety of mistakes. Mistakes as insignificant as misspellings in a report, to as serious as overlooking or misperceiving a key issue or theme in a presentation or analysis.

Effective leaders know that the world is, in fact, moving at an ever-increasing rate. Like it or not, we must accept the reality that the rate of change is accelerating. Just consider the accelerating pace of innovation in any of a number of fields. Let's briefly review the history of a basic form of communication—the evolution of the written word from scrawlings on a cave wall to book form.

In the beginning (sounds Biblical, doesn't it?), there was only word of mouth. Communication took place by speaking and singing—also through drawings. But, let's fast forward several thousand or million years, depending on how you perceive the evolution of mankind. Eventually, alphabets were codified and then words were written, first on rock walls and then on parchment. The parchment was later refined so it could be rolled into a scroll for safekeeping and easier transportation.

Centuries later, during the Roman era, binding of pages was invented, a necessary precursor to the modern-day book, eventually replacing scrolls. That made reading and transporting the written word much easier. Then, around a thousand years later, movable type was invented so books could be printed instead of being handwritten. In fact, later on, after the printing press was invented, scores of books and later thousands could be produced in a single year. Perhaps every printer's guild back then was the collective Henry Ford of its time. Can you say (relatively speaking, since relatively few could read) "mass production"?

Then only a half a millennium after Gutenberg's invention of the printing press, the world moved from printed books to the Internet and, at the beginning of the twenty-first century, to books printed on demand. Wow! Only a nanosecond later (in historical terms) the digital book was born in various iterations via Kindle, the Nook, and the iPad, among others. On reflection, we see the evolution of the written word grow at warp speed following the invention of the printing press. And now, digital readers are eclipsing the printing press, the prior tipping point in the journey of the written word. How interesting, we might note, that the technology that created the book has morphed into a technology that, at the least, is shaking the foundation of the bound paper book. A classic form of creative destruction. And, how even more interesting that it seems to be happening at the speed of light! Or, does it feel that way because it only is happening at our personal speed of light?

This increase in the rate of change of the rate of change, the so-called second derivative, can make us feel as if information, all of technology, is growing at warp speed. It's almost as if information is expanding at the same rate as the expansion of our universe. Not only does it feel that way, from our earthly perspective perhaps it is! Clearly, the digital age has unleashed perhaps the most exponential expansion of access to knowledge in our history. But as with most technologies, it can be a blessing and a bane—does nuclear power come to mind?

Similarly, the Internet (the precursor to the evolving age of the digital book), if harnessed well, is an incredibly beneficial tool. Clearly, the Internet has been instrumental in increasing productivity. But, does the seemingly speed-of-light expansion of fingertip-available-knowledge really help us to know more? The Internet is always available to unleash information beguiling and enchanting us to learn more, to explore more, and, to rely on it more. Doesn't it seek to addict the unwary, disguising its enchantment in the form of entertainment, information, socializing, or otherwise? Perhaps the Internet is an inanimate ever-growing tree of too much information, and while its alluring fruit is not forbidden, indigestion from information overload awaits those who overindulge. Is the ever-increasing knowledge available through the Internet creating a vortex beckoning and luring us into it, deeper and deeper the more we use it? In fact, the more we use it, the more we tend to rely on it. For Internet-addicts, it can be a black hole of digital density seemingly requiring inter-galactic counter-force in order to escape. Hasn't the BlackBerry or iPhone become permanently attached to the hand of too many of the Millennial Generation? The Internet seems to offer us the antithetical proposition of either too much or not enough information. If we embrace the Internet, we risk being overwhelmed by its wealth of information, perhaps undercutting our ability to make productive use of it. Yet, if we avoid the Internet altogether, we are disadvantaged by not enough knowledge. If much of life is about balance, why should our effective harnessing of the Internet require less skill?

Because so much information is available to us through the Internet, some of us allow ourselves to believe we can now attain perfection. Perfection in our knowledge of a subject, perfection in our relationships, perfection in anything we attempt to do. As T.S. Eliot lamented, "Where is the life we have lost in living? Where is the wisdom we have lost in knowledge? Where is the knowledge we have lost in information?" If perfection has become a goal achievable by mere mortals, what does the oft-repeated phrase "perfection is the saboteur of success" mean, and why is it so often disregarded by those who know little, and so respected (even feared) by those who evolve in their knowledge and wisdom? Why is the attempt to attain perfection our enemy and why is it so hard to learn this seemingly contradictory truth?

Perhaps Einstein captured the essence of the "perfection equation" best by comparing a more knowledgeable person and a less knowledgeable person to a pair of circles. The radius of each circle (half of its diameter, or height) represents a person's innate ability to acquire knowledge, or the "reach" of their intellect. The area of the circle represents a person's accumulated factual knowledge, while the perimeter of a person's "knowledge circle" represents the boundary of this knowledge.

Let's compare the two individuals' circles. Say, the radius of the less knowledgeable person's circle is half that of the more knowledgeable person's circle (2 inches and 4 inches respectively). From this we can calculate that the total of the less knowledgeable person's factual knowledge, represented by the area of his or her circle, is roughly 12.56 inches (πr^2), while the area of the more knowledgeable person's circle, or the totality of their accumulated knowledge, is approximately 50 inches. This raises the question: why doesn't the more intelligent person know exactly twice as much (as opposed to approximately four times as much) as the less intelligent person based on their twice-as-strong intellectual reach? Why do they know so much more? Is it because knowledge becomes self-generating and builds upon itself? Let's analyze.

A more powerful intellect is able to acquire more knowledge. But isn't there also a snowball effect? A geometric growth which occurs by virtue of the deductive processes. As more knowledge is accumulated and more knowledge is internally generated (deduced) by the mind, the two chain-react. Existing and new knowledge bounce off one another to create ever-new knowledge—a sort of spontaneous combustion of creativity—resulting in an increase in knowledge. Just as this creative combustion works for the individual, it also works when a group of individuals work together. We brainstorm internally, but we also brainstorm externally when several individuals work collectively. Individual deduction or communal brainstorming—both generate new knowledge, creating new knowns from the current knowns.

Another way of understanding our sense of the more knowledgeable (versus less knowledgeable) person is offered by another perspective on Einstein's circle. Consider his circle metaphor using the perimeter or circumference as describing the boundary of one's knowledge. As Einstein pointed out, just as important as what a person knows is what they know that they do not know or, to borrow from Donald H. Rumsfeld, a former Secretary of Defense, their "known unknowns." Each of us only knows what is within our circle of knowledge. Conversely, we do not know the information outside our circle. Einstein argued that we can determine how much a person knows that they do not know by examining the perimeter of his or her circle at which points he or she "touches" what lies beyond their circle of knowledge in their "zone of ignorance." Euclidean geometry teaches us that the circumference of a circle (the measurement of its perimeter) is $2\pi r$. Accordingly, the perimeter of the less knowledgeable person's circle, with a radius of 2 inches, is approximately 12.56 inches, while the length of the edge of the more knowledgeable person's circle, his perimeter or boundary, with a radius of 4 inches, is 25.12 inches. Since the perimeter of the more knowledgeable person's circle is longer than that of the less knowledgeable person's circle, Einstein deduces that the more knowledgeable person better recognizes their relative lack of knowledge compared to the factually less knowledgeable person. Why? Because according to Einstein, the more knowledgeable person "touches" more of their "zone of ignorance." In other words, the more knowledgeable person is more knowledgeable not just because he has greater factual knowledge at his disposal, but because he better grasps the concept that, no matter how large his knowledge base becomes, his knowledge will only encompass a miniscule fraction of all knowledge. In essence, the more knowledgeable person better knows what he does not know.

Based on this, one might speculate that while wisdom (or knowing that one does not know) can never be equated with factual knowledge, there is a link. The bigger one's "circle of knowledge" grows, the more one becomes aware of how little he or she knows. Why? Because his base of known unknowns grows with greater knowledge. Or, as perhaps the most knowledgeable person in history, Socrates, said "All I know is that I know nothing."

The correlate is that fools rush in where wise men fear to go. The more knowledgeable person better understands that the quest for perfection is a "fool's errand." Just compare the teenager who "knows it all" to the same person 30 years later whose greater knowledge, maturity, and wisdom causes them, at the same time, to know much more, yet to know less. The quest for knowledge is never-ending, yet, perfection will always elude us.

To sum up, according to Einstein, in our example, the more knowledgeable person is significantly more ignorant than the less knowledgeable person. With apologies to former Secretary of Defense, Donald Rumsfeld, see diagram below which depicts a square (not intended to be to scale) as constituting all knowledge.

Shaded Area Constitutes All Knowledge

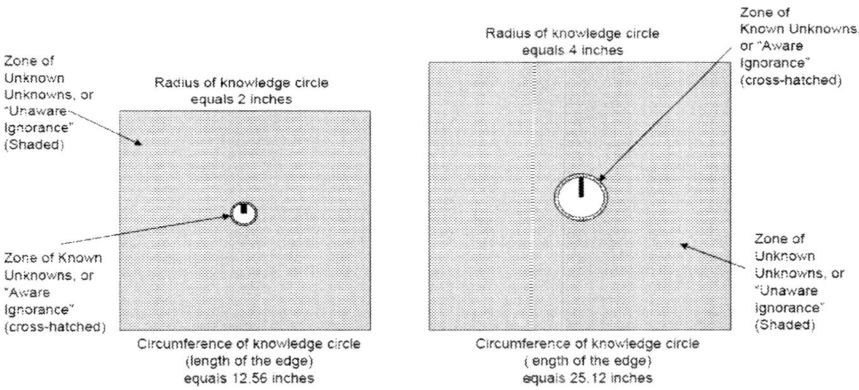

So, you ask, what do the speed of light, the evolution of the printed word, the allure of the Internet, and the quest for perfection have in common, and what do they have to do with leadership? Lots. Let's see.

Each, in its own way, is an opiate. Each in its own way seeks to master us, control us. To some people, lack of speed means failure. But is that true? Ask Aesop's tortoise and hare. How often do we rush a project or just speak too fast to mask our fears and insecurities?

When I was a music student learning to play the drums, I thought I mastered many of the rudiments. At the next lesson, I played the practice pieces quickly. I thought I would be praised.

But my music teacher stopped me and said, "If you can play it well, you can play it well slowly. I want to see you execute each stroke, each beat, with proper form and cadence."

I was initially stunned. But as I played more slowly, as my teacher demanded, I began to see errors the untrained ear would miss when I played faster. Had my teacher not forced me to slow down, I might never have mastered the key rudimentary skills of percussion.

Yet, we sometimes equate lack of speed, a slower pace, with losing, or, at least, not winning. Even worse, we see it as failure. Obviously, in many pursuits, like that 60-meter dash, speed counts. Yet, speed also maims and even kills, whether in a narcotic, vehicular, or more abstract form. It just depends on the context.

Why do we confuse speed with success? Aren't we all too often driven by our completion complex and desire to get things done causing us to sometimes misplay the rudiments or skip a beat.

When a task is left uncompleted, we may feel we aren't working fast enough. Not having finished, we must grapple with our completion complex—the desire to finish things, get things "done and over with." We grapple with the weight and time-factor of other items clogging or bogging our to-do list, so we decide to proceed faster—sometimes too fast—as we try to reach or exceed our personal speed limit to get these tasks out of the way.

The effective leader can sense when others go too fast. Effective leaders recognize when subordinates are "red-lining" the engine in their head. Effective leaders help others balance the time demands and deadlines of the job, and motivate others to reach for, but not exceed, their speed limits. They understand the size of the wheels and width of the tracks, so to speak, of their subordinates, as well as the power of their engines. Effective leaders "gauge the gauge" of each of their subordinates. Effective leaders help their associates achieve their maximum speed without inefficient vibration and, in all cases, without derailing.

The evolution of the printed word, if plotted on a graph, would bear little resemblance to a normal growth curve. Perhaps when the speed of growth begins to accelerate exponentially, the growth line or curve somehow seems to invert upon itself, almost as if it is creating a new beginning. It is interesting that a change from "in the beginning" to "a new beginning" takes us from the comfortably Biblical to an adventurous and scary Sci-Fi.

The debut of the digital book marked the beginning of slower growth, maybe worse, of the printed book, even bookstores themselves. As this marvelous creation develops, it also destroys—a healthy, creative clearing away of the underbrush of older technology for the next advance. Effective leaders well know that change is perhaps the only constant. They are vigilant to detect those parts of the here-and-now that may be surpassed and even destroyed by future developments. Effective leaders understand the here-and-now is under constant attack and is, in some respects, constantly eroding. Effective leaders are always on the lookout for the "enemies" of the status quo. They seek them out. They are the next generation of ideas, inventions, gadgets, and techniques that will surely come despite the naysayers and fear mongers. Effective leaders embrace the new, untested, or unknown. They understand the comfort zone for them and their subordinates is an insidious affirmation of the status quo.

The Internet is perhaps the greatest facilitator of the erosion of the here-and-now. It is both a vast archive of the past and the locus of an immeasurable stream of up-to-the-second speculation about what the future will bring. It is all too easy to fall into the trap of ceaseless reflection on the events of the past or anxious anticipation of the events of the future. But only if we allow ourselves to!

We walk in the street—worse yet, we drive our cars—while our mind is light years away. The tripartite division of existence, into the past, present, and future causes a rip. A rip in our being—a rip in our here-and-now. And, the more we divorce our mind from our body, the greater the rip in our personal here-and-now. Sometimes, all too dangerously.

Because we dream, because we all ruminate, at least some of the time (perhaps all of the time), we allow ourselves too often to slip into a past or future moment. We allow our thoughts to separate our mind from the place and time of our body. So we attend a meeting, and ruminate on portions of the conversation or negotiation as we drive home. Perhaps we focus on a part of the meeting when we were caught off guard by a quick-witted response that left us speechless or, worse yet, a well-placed jab that we were unprepared to parry. So we play the sequence over and over in our mind, usually re-scripted to end the way we would have liked had we then responded with the perfect response (or, if in Paris, l'esprit de l'escalier). Ruminating is not healthy. Forgive the other person and let the incident dissolve as you bathe it with your grace.

If we are driving, it's dangerous to ruminate, but at least our eyes are on the road even though our mind is somewhere else. On the other hand, when we use our digital devices while we are with other people (or, worse, when driving), we take both our mind and our eyes off the road, away from the present moment. That action conveys bad messages to the other person: You are bored, or something else is more important, or you just want to be somewhere else or with someone else. Is our excessive usage of the Internet turning us into "inter-gnats"? Will taking our eyes off the here-and-now road crush us on the windshield of life?

Effective leaders understand that a key element of success is focus. Few initiatives require brilliance. However, everything requires sufficient focus to reach the finish line, to complete the matter at hand. Effective leaders must inculcate the desire and ability to live in the present. They understand that living and working in the present enables each subordinate to reach their optimum and that their optimum, regardless of level, is usually all that is required.

Perfection is the bane of every leader. How many deadlines were missed in the name of perfection? How many parts of a project were skipped or short-shifted in the quest for perfection of other parts, regardless of relative importance? Most things in life simply require timely completion. An application for college, an analysis of a competitor, a report, or a legal brief—few, if any, efforts require a grade of 100. Most projects and efforts just need a grade of A. Better a 97 than a 90, but in most cases, just a low A will do, so long as it's timely. In fact, if only the Creator is perfect, is it not arrogant to demand perfection from ourselves? While it may be a good trait to strive for perfection, it's no doubt divine to recognize our humanity and accept less. As the commercial for Korean Air advises, pursue excellence (not *be* excellent).

Effective leaders know that few, if any, circumstances in life allow the luxury of taking all the time one would like. The good news is that few, if any, require that much time. In fact, effective leaders know that some issues require no time at all. Zero! Left unattended, such as the request from an associate for a decision the associate must learn to make on her own, they often resolve themselves. On the other hand, most tasks do require focus and effort, although we rarely have the chance to apply as much effort or time as we would like.

Effective leaders learn how to make decisions with less than all available information. The best leaders teach their senior subordinates (their captains and potential heirs apparent) to do the same. While not optimum, effective leaders—due to deadlines, real or artificial—are often required to make decisions on less than complete information. They know they have *enough* information to make a decision, but they also know more could be obtained to make a better-informed decision if there were no deadlines and competitive pressures. But deadlines and competitive pressures almost always exist. That's life. What's the point in making the near-perfect bid to purchase a competitor if the bid is too late? Say, after an agreement was inked by the competitor to sell to another company and the agreement contained a prohibitively costly break-up fee. What's the benefit in delivering the near-perfect report to a client on an untimely basis if its delivery is made after the client was so frustrated, annoyed, and unnerved from the delay, that he sought the report from your competitor, or simply ended the relationship because of the anxiety?

Effective leaders understand that completion on a timely basis almost always equals success, and that untimely completion, even with a near-perfect product, often spells failure, or at least something less than success, because it is tinged by the disappointment, frustration, or anxiety of the recipient.

The speed of light is as elusive as perfection. Effective leaders understand that the quest for perfection is a protective blanket for the insecure and inexperienced. Hence, effective leaders instill the basics. They often take a page from the coaching style of Vince Lombardi, legendary former head football coach of the Green Bay Packers. Teams win with basic, well-executed blocking, tackling, and offensive plays, and focus is the shortest route to the end zone of success. Effective leaders help subordinates learn to clear their mind, mentally block out distractions, and seek 100% focus on the task at hand. Operating at warp speed may just propel us into a personal black hole. Perhaps that's what happened to Aesop's hare who was trying to race at a hare's speed of light, only to be distracted (and overcome by the arrogance of ego) and eclipsed by the slower and steady tortoise. Effective leaders practice the teachings of children's bedtime stories from time to time, too! They live the fable perhaps not as the tortoise and the hare, but rather as the earthly success versus the ethereal search for perfection. Effective leaders strive for and seek excellence. They leave concepts of light speed to the scientists and perfection to the Creator.

- Speed can be a blessing, but it can also maim or kill. It maims or kills a quick but not fully accurate response, or a fast analysis that lacked full development.
- While the world sometimes moves at warp speed, effective leaders never allow themselves or their subordinates to exceed their personal speed limits.
- The Internet can bombard us at seemingly warp speed. The Internet can be beguilingly addictive. The Internet is a saboteur of focus.
- Effective leaders always preach focus and concentration.
- Effective leaders are masters of the "here and now." Their effectiveness is much a function of how much of their time they can

spend in the present moment. They work to avoid distraction, rumination and mental wandering.

- Effective leaders understand how little they know—they advance new initiatives and new ideas carefully but confidently.
- Effective leaders understand the difference between brainstorming and daydreaming. They know daydreams are generally shattered by the harshness of the return to reality. But, they also know, counterintuitively, daydreams can be the basis for epiphanies.
- Effective leaders are wary of "hare-like" employees. Too often their speed is an attempt to mask insecurity, fear, and ignorance.
- Effective leaders understand the simple equation that timely completion equals success. They know that equation usually is shattered by those who quest perfection.

CHAPTER 9

LEADERSHIP AND THE "REDO"

What if it were possible for us to travel so fast that we could arrive where we started earlier than when we departed? In other words, travel back in time. Or, as the sportscasters would say, "hit the instant replay button."

Aren't all of our "do-overs" restarts? How many times have we thought, "I wish I could do that again and make it better?" A restart, we imagine, is the holy grail to reach perfection. How often have we wished for a second chance—a completely new beginning or, perhaps, just an adjustment? Don't we all secretly wish we could repeat our steps until we make things perfect, or just get them more right?

But would we have actually defeated our objective? At what point do we defeat our goal, undermine our purpose, by somehow losing sight of the goal line as we lose ourselves in a quest for perfection? What if our lives began to resemble a series of retakes? Might we not find ourselves in a time helix of never-ending retakes as we work to reach perfection? Can we ever reach perfection, or would we just keep working to improve our last effort?

Retakes are a seemingly positive rationale to justify delay. Retakes to a fault are, in a sense, the most insidious form of distraction. We all recognize the obviously negative distractions. You may have read that employees of the Securities and Exchange Commission were found to be spending significant portions of their workdays surfing pornographic sites on the Internet. Clearly a negative distraction. But don't most of us check our e-mail frequently? At what point does checking e-mail, stock quotes, Facebook, and the like morph from a welcome and perhaps well-needed diversion into a series of negative distractions? At what point does this behavior become an addiction?

Every foray on the Internet for any reason other than one's current focus is a distraction. We all understand the seductive nature of the Internet; in fact, we often yearn for that diversion when we just need or want a break from the matter at hand. Because we chose it, we think we control it, as opposed to the third-party distraction of, say, a co-worker entering our office unannounced either to chat or seek the answer to a question.

The redo, because it's fueled by the desire to get things right, may be the worst distraction of all, bred of the insecurity that our work product or effort is just not good enough. Perhaps, by extension, that we are just not good enough. Or, fear may immobilize us as we seek to avoid the assumed negative response to less than acceptable, certainly less than perfect, results. We finished the work, but our insecurity boils up to convince us it needs to be better. Hence, the restart. Hence, the delay. The delay in completing this task, and the delay in starting the next task. Some of us can't let go of our fear. We're compelled to dwell on the current project, compelled to seek a 100%, an A+.

Of course, sometimes restarts or redo's are appropriate. We may discover a new fact or issue, or see things from a new perspective, all of which require a redo. I'm not referring to that circumstance—that is the hallmark of success. No, I'm referring to a job well done, but nevertheless being reworked, refined, re-edited, re-"whatevered," because of a need to try to make it perfect.

Here's an interesting redo many of us have undertaken. Perhaps we were doing a good job but we lost our focus several times as we dealt with interruptions causing stops and starts. As a result, we lost the continuum and we're just not sure it's sufficiently completed. After the restart is completed, we find we had reached the A level and that it was already good enough. That's also a healthy redo, because it's based not on insecurity or fear, but conscientiousness. We knew we had been distracted and needed to make sure that the continuum was intact and the work was not inferior as a result of stops and starts.

There have always been distractions, but since the very late twentieth century (about the last 25 years) distractions are ubiquitous. Thanks to the Internet, we evolved from actively seeking an entertaining distraction to pushing a button or two on our laptops. In fact, we can now suffocate ourselves with distractions. Is it any wonder that many Internet users are becoming "inter-gnats"? The world and all of its information is literally at our fingertips. We need effective controllers within ourselves to avoid distraction.

It's just like the cadmium rods that were used in the first nuclear reactors. When nuclear reactors were first built, the engineers used cadmium rods to control the process. The rods were inserted into the reactor to decelerate the nuclear reaction and were removed in order to accelerate the process. But where are our cadmium rods? How do we control our use of the Internet? We have them. They are invisibly within us.

How do leaders teach focus? How do they teach subordinates to avoid the sweet calls of delay? What must leaders do to help subordinates remain focused, abstain from distraction, and avoid delay? How do subordinates resist the attractive siren songs of distractions? How do they avoid the constant beckoning of their power and beauty?

Effective leaders allow subordinates to drink the elixirs of completion and decision. In fact, the very best encourage fully imbibing in the libation. To understand what is necessary as a predicate, we must first understand why leaders offer the elixirs. But we must also understand why other leaders may offer only if asked, and why still others refuse to offer the elixir under any circumstances.

In the leadership context, a combination of character (integrity) and maturity (the wisdom from age and experience) will create a context in which subordinates will seek advice, acknowledge errors, and yearn for growth. The by-product of those efforts is almost always an enhancement of their inner security. Why? Because subordinates almost always seek advice if they do not fear asking, acknowledge errors if they do not fear embarrassment, and yearn for growth if they do not fear sabotage.

Many leaders offer advice, but all too often in a demeaning or inconvenienced manner thereby subliminally conveying the message, "Don't ask again—you should have known the answer." That message is always wrong. On the other hand, when a subordinate asks for advice too often, effective leaders recognize they must help them make their own decisions.

Which brings us to leaders who address error in an embarrassing manner; of course, they are the less effective. Effective leaders use errors and mistakes as teaching tools, not lessons in their superiority. They praise the decision-makers and subordinates willing to challenge their inner security by acknowledging their error, adjusting, and moving forward more confidently. They never demean. As a result, the subordinate learns the equation of success. Error plus acknowledgement of error equals positive adjustment which yields success. The win-win formula of life, unless you somehow believe that we all should get it right the first time.

With the advice and adjustment legs of leadership in place, the third leg virtually develops by itself. The yearning for personal and professional growth just needs the warmth of positive sunlight and the nourishment of fresh water. The effective leader need do quite little, sometimes no more than getting out of the way, both literally and figuratively. Effective leaders do not let personal desires distract them and overcome doing other than what is in the best interest of the organization. Sometimes, the shortest step is the longest and most painful, the effective leader's little pas de deux to the side, thereby making room for subordinates to grow.

- We all need to recognize when the conscientiousness of a redo or a rework of a project morphs into excessive delay.
- Effective leaders understand the difference between healthy delay and idea-killer, deal-killer delay.
- Effective leaders understand it's impossible to get things perfect—that decisions often need to be made with the information at hand, albeit incomplete.
- Effective leaders understand that mistakes are always best avoided, but when made create a learning experience by executing "a fix" or simply analyzing the flawed effort.

CHAPTER 10

LEADERSHIP—AND THE LAW OF UNINTENDED EXPECTATIONS

When subordinates understand the task, really get it, they are more likely to complete it successfully. Effective leaders understand that hearing a sentence start with the phrase "I thought you meant . . ." is a leadership failure. Not the failure of the subordinate. When less effective leaders blame the subordinate, they are subconsciously blaming themselves. Effective leaders take responsibility for any misunderstanding so that then they can seek the basis for the lack of understanding.

The bases for misunderstanding come in many flavors. Sometimes, the leader may have misspoken. Perhaps the leader spoke too fast or wasn't clear in the instructions or guidance. Perhaps the subordinate wasn't up to the task and didn't really understand the scope of the project, its depth, complexity, or importance. Perhaps the subordinate perceived the project to be of secondary importance or, even worse, just a notch above "make-work." Perhaps the subordinate was preoccupied with another task and couldn't clear his mind. Perhaps, the subordinate was just overwhelmed by fear of meeting with the leader.

It really doesn't matter why the response (read: the completed project) fell short of the leader's expectations. All that matters is that it fell short. Whenever the work falls below the leader's expectations, effective leaders accept the responsibility. They accept the element of failure, their failure, when the response of a subordinate is below their expectation. Effective leaders convey expectations with clarity. Yet, even more important, they make sure the expectation they have is mirrored in the mind of their subordinate. Effective leaders seek congruent expectations, not dueling expectations.

But how can a leader impart a clear understanding of his expectation? It's simple to do, but difficult to do well. Why? Because it requires the leader to make sure that what he has said is understood by his subordinate exactly as he intended. We all tend to more readily hear things not as they are, but as we are—filtered by our knowledge, experience, and expectations.

As a result, to reach a confluence of expectations, leaders are often required to exercise many leadership skills. More so, and sometimes even harder, it requires the leader to neutralize his ego, disregard his superior position, and deal with the subordinate on a peer-to-peer level. Why? Because to do otherwise invites a failure of communication, and failed communication is one of the key predicates to the realization of unintended expectations—expectations below what was sought and required.

But why does a leader's ego so easily pave the way to unintended expectations? It's simple. A strain of virulent ego, when exhibited by a leader, usually causes the subordinate to develop a case of "question-a-phobia"—the fear of asking a clarifying or confirmatory question. When subordinates are bombarded by a leader's ego, they tend to want to escape from the leader's presence. Certainly, not admit their lack of understanding. They want to escape before they are demeaned, mocked, or otherwise belittled by the leader. It doesn't even matter whether the actions of the leader are, in fact, demeaning, mocking, or otherwise belittling. All that matters is the subordinate's perception that the leader's response will be negative: negative facial expression such as the rolling of the eyes, or a tone in the leader's response which broadcasts to all the world that the leader is disappointed, or worse. And why would a subordinate make a clarifying comment or ask a clarifying question if the expected response will be demeaning or just expose his ignorance in an embarrassing way?

Of course, effective leaders know that without clarifying comments or questions, they can't be sure they and their subordinates share the same expectations, or to use a "double bromide," are "on all fours on the same page." Accordingly, effective leaders know they must draw out comments and questions about the tasks in order to be certain the project is perceived by the subordinate exactly as perceived by the leader.

Is it any wonder that many leaders conclude the delivery of an assignment to their subordinates by asking, "Any questions?" But is that enough? When there is no response or the response is no, what should the effective leader do? There are two basic choices.

The first is to simply say okay and end the meeting in which the assignment was given. That choice is a good one if the leader knows the subordinate really grasps the assignment and expectations. It's also a good one if the leader has the confidence in the subordinate to know that the associate will ask questions if they arise. But, is it a good leadership policy to assume? Or, do these assumptions pave the way for the famous *Odd*

Couple television series quote when Felix says to Oscar, "When you assume you are likely to make an 'ass of you and me' (ass-u-me)."

On the other hand, perhaps the better basic choice is to make sure the subordinate really grasps the leader's expectations—grasps them upfront, at the beginning of the task. Why risk the subordinate heading for Chicago when the expected destination was Springfield, the capital of Illinois? When teachers finish a lesson, they ask if there are any questions. The best teachers ignore the inevitable silence and search the faces of their students for that look of confusion. And, when they find it, the best repeat the most difficult parts of the lesson.

The same successful formula applies to all effective leaders. Use the simple device of confirming expectation by inviting the subordinate (the student) to explain his understanding of the task. Invite the response in an ego-free manner with a true desire to make sure the subordinate really gets it. Some leaders won't take the extra time. Others think the exercise is demeaning to the subordinate, or fear it will be perceived that way. The first is the lazy way out, or the surfacing of ego. The second is a poor excuse for the leader's inability to question the subordinate in a positive manner.

It's always worth taking the scant additional time. How often has an extra 5–10 minutes saved hours, even days? So, the real leadership quality is to draw out the subordinate's understanding of the task in an ego-free, non-demeaning manner. The exercise is complicated if the subordinate, for whatever reason, thinks the request to confirm the understanding is demeaning. Effective leaders must overcome the subordinate's ego (as well as their own). Perhaps the subordinate is insecure or remembers past instances when the leader failed to control his ego and, in fact, was demeaning. Let's face it, no leader is perfect. Now and again we all let our ego slip out and offend others. Now is the time for every leader to bury his ego with grace.

So what does the effective leader do? What techniques are available to the effective leader to assure no unintended expectations? Once the leader buries his ego, the second choice is assured mutual understanding. For example, the effective leader might suggest that he is not certain he has fully explained all the elements of the assignment. He might even suggest that he wants to make sure he covered the task completely. Even better, that he'd like to brainstorm the task to refine and improve it. Then, by asking the subordinate to relate his understanding and thoughts, the effective leader converts the conversation from one of leader-to-subordinate to a partnering relationship where two colleagues (one senior to the other) are collaborating to further define and refine the task.

And is this interchange not a collaboration? Shouldn't all interchanges—between parents and children, peers, friends, colleagues—all be collaborations? By partnering with the subordinate, the effective leader accomplishes so much. Partnering allows the leader to extend the hand of compliment and trust to the subordinate by implicitly acknowledging the value of the subordinate's input. In addition, partnering creates a membrane through which the leader's instructions are filtered in a manner which allows the leader to hear the echo of what he said and thought. It doesn't matter how it's interpreted or repeated or perceived by the subordinate. What does matter is the leader's facilitation of the feedback to allow his thoughts to be re-crystallized through the perception of his subordinate. What must ensue, with the leader's ego neutralized and the subordinate's fears and insecurities allayed by the implied trust and confidence of the leader, is a synthesis of thoughts and ideas. A synthesis of expectations. The gold medal platform for a successful task or project.

Now, let's fast forward to the subordinate's work product. Given the time invested by the leader to assure his expectations would be met, how does an effective leader deal with underperformance?

One approach is to avoid using the same subordinate for the next assignment, but that is not what an effective leader would, or should, first decide to do. Why? Because abandonment is not leadership. Ignoring a problem with an associate is failed leadership and often cruel. Not addressing a problem is abdication of leadership. But, far worse are the psychological and emotional negative impacts of ignoring a problem subordinate through isolation and avoidance. Everyone involved suffers. The leader suffers knowing he is just hoping the problem will disappear. Probably hoping the subordinate will get the message and resign. The organization suffers as the "space" for a growing associate or new hire is clogged by the current hire. But most of all, the subordinate suffers. He suffers perhaps in the cruelest of ways. As discussed in Chapter 3, he suffers the anxieties from what I call the "death by a thousand pinpricks." The failing subordinate is seldom capable of accepting his inability to perform at the required level. Anxiety grows from continuing avoidance and isolation. Avoidance and isolation first emanating from the leader, but even finally from colleagues.

So what must the effective leader do? Effective leaders don't expect perfection. Rather, they expect and accept flaws. What they seek is a striving for excellence. The decision matrix for whether to terminate the subordinate is not "acceptable versus a non-acceptable" analysis; rather, it's a curve analysis. Is the subordinate moving forward on an acceptable growth curve? If the answer is yes and the subordinate is exceeding minimum performance standards, the employee should qualify for training and development.

It is reasonable to expect that minimum standards must be achieved and then exceeded. When performance is below-goal and growth is elusive, termination should quickly follow. Tolerance is a trait to be admired, except when it becomes a pair of leadership handcuffs preventing termination. Retaining underperformers, whether in the name of kindness or sympathy or politics, is just a rationale for failed leadership.

When political correctness becomes a rationale for undue tolerance, for inaction, everyone loses. Effective leaders well understand that organizational culture matters and that fairness must prevail. Yet, life does not always allow for fairness, as perceived by all, to win out. Effective leaders always treat subordinates with kindness and compassion, even when situational dynamics call for a result that may not seem fair.

Perhaps the most deleterious unintended consequence arises from a leader's attempt to be fair when the right thing to do seems either unfair, harsh, or even cruel. Termination of a subordinate would seem to qualify as all three. Fairness, of course, is always in the eyes of the beholder. With so many eyes in an organization, a push in the direction of one beholder's eyes often creates imbalances, injustices, and inequities in the eyes of many others. Effective leaders are charged with making effective decisions. All they can do is act in such a way that the consequences of their actions and their expectations are intended.

- It's so hard for us to understand what the other person is saying or really intending. It's hard because we process what we think we've heard. It's hard because what we say or hear and how we say or hear it translates in each of our brains as a function of our individual backgrounds, experiences, and the frames of reference we bring to any conversation. Things are not as they are, things present themselves to us as we are.
- Effective leaders train their subordinates to hear and digest and confirm what they think they heard and how they understand it so they never have to later say "I thought you meant . . ."
- Effective leaders train themselves to reinforce and confirm what they have said to others in order to eliminate misunderstanding.

Effective leaders take the extra time to confirm what they have said to another or what another has said to them.

- Effective leaders know that effective communication is best assured by confirmation.
- Effective leaders seek for all to be on the same wavelength—never to take comprehension and understanding for granted.
- Effective leaders know that sloppy listening and misperception are the ingredients that undermine understanding. Effective leaders do not leave room for misperception or misunderstanding.

CHAPTER 11

LEADERSHIP AND THE SON OF AMRAM

Leaders must live on a mountaintop, whether that mountaintop is the helm of a ship, the flight deck of an aircraft, or the office of the CEO. Mountaintops are, in fact, the perfect perch. It is only from that vantage point that leaders can see to all horizons. But, equally important as the breadth of a leader's mountaintop view is the real-world vista below the mountaintop, a real world filled with dangers. There are flaws and dangers lurking in the valleys and fields of everyday organizational life—perhaps a jagged rock-face, a hidden waterfall, or a river with many dead-end streams (read, for example, a disgruntled employee).

This dual living style to see both the stars and mountaintops beyond yet at the same time the dangers below is how leaders must position themselves. And it's exactly what effective leaders do.

Leaders are charged with the responsibility of setting direction and then understanding the strengths and weaknesses of their organization in order to effect execution. Effective leaders find ways to utilize organizational strengths, while overcoming or shoring up weaknesses.

What makes leadership so difficult? Why are truly effective leaders so rare? For one, they must accept a degree of solitude while, at the same time, seek the input and advice of others. Solitude can be a frequent visitor and always seems to pay leaders a visit when the decisions that can really make a difference are upon them. There is no escaping the harsh loneliness of the phrase, "The buck stops here." However, a solitary view begets a solitary understanding of the unique circumstances in which an organization finds itself at any given moment in time. While a leader can share his thoughts, ideas, and vision, he cannot entirely share his view. No one else in the organization can synthesize all the input from the same perspective as the leader. The leader's mountaintop view and perspective is his alone. Eagles' nests are well protected and far from dangers and distractions below, whether friend or foe.

The leader stands, at the same time, with his organization but also between the organization's current status quo and the future he envisions.

How lonely a position! He seeks constantly to move his organization forward in the hope of fulfilling his vision for growth, while having to neutralize the naysayers, not to mention the laws of nature, particularly that persnickety law of inertia, about which Sir Isaac Newton wrote—that a body at rest tends to remain at rest unless a force (read: the positive, yet destructive creativity of a leader) is exerted upon that body.

Loneliness is an inescapable by-product of leadership. How can it be otherwise? All of the leader's subordinates live in the valley below, a valley filled with desire for personal achievement, and the concomitant competitive instincts, jealousies, complaints, and criticisms.

Leadership is lonely, but effective leaders understand it cannot be isolating. Hence, all effective leaders spend time in the fields and valleys below. To do otherwise would infect a leader with the ignorance of isolation. How else but by descending from the mountaintop could an effective leader gauge the difficulty of the terrain he must cross to reach the next mountaintop? It is only at the lower altitudes that a leader can grasp the ever-changing mosaic, his constituents and constituencies. New initiatives may be conceived and envisioned on the mountaintop, perhaps planned there as well, but they are carried out in the fields and valleys.

It is only in the valley that the effective leader can be the "face that launches 1000 ships." Only in the fields and valleys a leader can motivate his subordinates to implement initiatives and strategies. While a leader can return to the mountaintop to study his strategy and the beauty of his vision, that vision is doomed to weaken or even fail if he dismisses the field conditions which invariably require adjustments and course corrections. What's more, "once begun may be half done," as the saying goes, but initiatives, just like football games, are usually won or lost in the fourth quarter. Accordingly, effective leaders understand that once the initiative is launched, frequent and extended returns to the mountaintop may cause erosion and decay of the initiative. Every initiative demands follow-through. Effective leaders know initiatives take more than vision, they require follow-through. Follow-through is the necessary ingredient to overcome Newton's second law. Without follow-through, the corporate body will simply come to rest, overcome by the forces of fear and status quo.

An effective leader must be the conduit between his vision and implementation. Conduits are effective only if they conduct. Otherwise, they are not conduits at all. Effectiveness, effective leadership, is a function of connectivity.

Hence, effective leaders are constantly descending to the valley below. The lifeblood of an organization, with all of its imperfections and flaws, is in the valleys and fields below. It is in the field where the field changes must be made. It's virtually impossible to see the field problems from the mountaintop, just as it is for those in the field to readily grasp the view and vision from the mountaintop.

Effective leaders know that the perfect implementation they see on the mountaintop can never be replicated in the valleys and fields below. Real, everyday life just gets in the way. Whether it's the jury duty obligation of a key employee, the illness of an employee's family member, or perhaps nothing more than another's bad day.

These impediments, these natural imperfections and flaws, remind the effective leader that great vision is critical, but it's not enough. Great vision must be complemented with two dashes of kindness, three tablespoons of compassion, and generous helpings of the secret sauce of *esprit de corps* which must be constantly stirred to prevent it from congealing.

But, how does an effective leader create *esprit de corps*? What must a leader do or say to create the secret sauce? Money is a start but, by itself, never enough. *Esprit de corps* cannot be found in a paycheck. It can't be resuscitated at the end of every pay period. It needs to exist all the time. And, it needs to become self-generating.

Esprit de corps is the DNA of an organization. DNA is the special sauce of humans. DNA, or deoxyribonucleic acid, determines who we are and enables us to exist as we are. DNA exists, we think, just to make more of itself. The DNA of an organization, its *esprit de corps*, channels the organization into the leader's vision for growth. In a sense, effective leaders are the organization's RNA, converting and interpreting the organization's life source to its proteomic members, just as RNA, ribonucleic acid, delivers the messages of the body's DNA to the body's proteins. Effective leaders do not need to be biologists or physicists. The laboratory of life is not filled with Bunsen burners, test tubes, and the like. Effective leaders understand, however, that the chemical reaction in a laboratory is similar to the emotional or psychological reaction between two or more "agents" in an organization.

Hence, all effective leaders spend as much time as they can with their subordinates. Why there's even a current television series testifying to its importance. It's called "Undercover Boss." How better to really grasp the field conditions, the problems, and determine a way to overcome them than to work in the field as a field hand? What better way for a leader to understand what it takes to effect implementation? What better way to get straight answers than to observe and listen? Really observe and really listen, as just another co-worker. How else can an effective leader really hear and see the unvarnished reality of the day-to-day workings of his organization? What better way to truly understand what the job takes than to do it yourself or work with others to get the job done?

Effective leaders understand the "paperclip" syndrome. They know that if a paperclip remains, say, in a hallway or otherwise out in the open, and no one stops to pick it up, *esprit de corps*, in the smallest and seemingly inconsequential way, may be at risk. Some leaders will ask a subordinate to pick up the paperclip or ask why hasn't it been picked up. Effective leaders just pick it up themselves. No comment, no fanfare. Effective leaders pick up paperclips all the time. They never ask another. Eventually, they never have to ask.

And, so, as we conclude this chapter, we look to one of the great leaders of all time, the son of Amram. His mountaintop was high indeed. In fact, high enough to have the Creator's Ten Commandments revealed to him. At that very moment, he stood between the Creator and his people. He was the conduit for the Creator's vision of a code of conduct by which to live. Can you imagine that vision! But, remaining on the mountaintop in the glory of the Creator's vision left him isolated and solitary. How could he effectuate the Creator's vision without returning to the field and valleys below? He knew the thin air of the mountaintop may somehow abet the ability to see beautiful visions, but could also disintegrate them, lest they were able to flourish in the more oxygenated air below. So, he returned to his people and endured their complaints and criticisms. He understood that the status quo is the easy path. He understood, intuitively, Newton's first law. So he endured the hurts and the betrayals and remained in the fields and valleys below to develop the *esprit de corps* which eventually turned his people from worshipping idols and golden calves to a concept of a single, non-seeable Creator. Moses, Amram's second-born son. What a great leader!

- Effective leaders understand the loneliness of their top-of-the-ladder position.
- They understand the fear and anxiety in others created by their development of new initiatives.
- Effective leaders understand that decisions may be made from their perch atop the organization, but effective implementation is carried out in the field.

- Effective leaders must constantly work to impart their vision and then see to its execution given the reality of in-the-field conditions.
- Effective leaders are omnipresent bosses—their omnipresence pervades the organization via its *esprit de corps*.
- Effective leaders know *esprit de corps* is the special sauce they create or inherit. They also know it must be nurtured with a stir now and again to protect it from congealing.

CHAPTER 12

LEADERSHIP AND THE COMFORT ZONE

Comfort zones are so comfortable. Why? It's obvious. It's the zone in which whatever we are doing is something we've done before, know how to do, and are no doubt good at it. It's the place we strive to reach after undertaking a new task, a new challenge.

Every new task or challenge draws us out of our comfort zone. Our comfort zones were always challenged in school. Our teachers constantly asked us to take a new step, continue to master a subject, or start to learn a new one. We learned that growth was a continuum of reaching a comfort zone only to be challenged to leave its safety and confines as we started to master a new area of knowledge, or a new sport, perhaps acclimate to a new set of friends and students.

Some of us reveled at the challenge, at the new beginning. Others faced the change with trepidation. It's so nice and comfortable to recline in our La-Z-Boy and watch our favorite television programs. It's so relaxing and non-stressful to always be with old friends "where everybody knows your name."

Effective leaders understand that a key element of their charge is to challenge subordinates to leave their comfort zone. Even more important, to challenge themselves to leave their personal comfort zones.

Effective leaders always seek to refine and improve their organization's competencies while, at the same time, strive to develop new competencies. To do otherwise breeds stagnation. To do otherwise creates a prescription for staleness and eventual erosion. Nothing stays the same for long. Allowing an individual or an organization to remain in his or its comfort zone most assuredly begets stalling. And, just like an airplane, the laws of aerodynamics demand that a stalled aircraft eventually loses acceleration and lift, and descends to the ground in an uncontrollable downward spiral.

Organizations and individuals act much the same. Comfort zones are devoid of acceleration. Their forward movements are a vestige of the acceleration an organization or an individual mustered to master an area that is now comfortable.

Comfort is the nemesis of growth. Effective leaders always instill an ethic of asking all members of an organization to challenge themselves, including, most importantly, themselves.

Effective leaders constantly challenge themselves. They continually renovate their thought processes. Effective leaders know that just sticking with a past success can soften an organization's mindset. If a leader allows the past success to remain the goal, the organization starts to become cumbersome, overprotective, and foolishly risk-averse.

Effective leaders know that success, without new success, will eventually erode. As a result, they force themselves to leave their personal comfort zones by challenging themselves with new ideas, new solutions, and new directions, even at the risk of harm to their current success.

But how can a leader constantly instill a "refresher" into the organization? How can he open the windows and let the fresh air in? It's simple. Just follow the now-famous maxim of Avis Rent A Car Company. Just think that you are #2—try harder.

As we reacted to the Avis commercial, we saw a company striving to be #1, to be the best in its industry. We envisioned a smart, hungry company with a clear goal (presumably to be #1 in sales and profits).We envisioned a hard-charging leader urging the pursuit of excellence. Urging his reports to leave their comfort zones and work to put Avis at #1.

Yet, challenges to comfort zones, to the status quo, create disruptions, and disruptions create anxiety. To a subordinate, the anxiety may be a function of his belief that what he has mastered, what he is doing, just isn't good enough. That he just isn't good enough! That he may not succeed at a new task. Effective leaders understand the inherent disruptive nature of new initiatives, of demanding the mastery of new tasks. They know their challenge is to acknowledge the value of the comfort zones of their subordinates, while at the same time finding positive ways to move them into new growth areas and out of their comfort zones.

Let's examine Joe, member of a firm's marketing department. Let's assume he is quite successful in marketing (selling) the firm's products in a particular region or in a particular industry where his penetration and development of business has produced annual increases in sales while maintaining profit margins, despite his opening new accounts which often require special incentives to break into the account and dislodge or replace a competitor.

Let's further assume that Herb, another member of the marketing (sales) department, is not performing nearly as well. Let's further assume that Joe sells to information technology accounts while Herb sells to pharmaceutical accounts.

If the leader decides to shift Joe to Herb's area of responsibility, how should he do it? What if Herb didn't exist and selling to the pharmaceutical industry was an entirely new area of business for the company, an entirely new initiative?

What exactly is the leader asking of Joe, the successful subordinate? But to understand the "ask," effective leaders first make sure they really understand Joe's comfort zone.

Comfort zones come in many flavors. Joe's overall comfort level emanates from his success. But let's look at the constituent potential elements of Joe's comfort zone. Perhaps he has developed deep relationships with his subordinates or with his key customers. Perhaps it's his rhythm of travel—personal calls—and follow-ups via telephone and e-mail. Perhaps in Joe's world, he's "made it" and has no interest in developing further. Why should he take the risk? He's a mini-star already! Each of these comfort zone elements are potential saboteurs to Joe's growth. The known and comfortable are reliable friends. But the effective leader understands they are friendships of the status quo, like a TV show with predictable developments within the same theme, just as in *Cheers*, the TV series where everybody knows your name.

Joe's leader knows that really successful salespeople are rare. So, let's assume his leader neither wants to transfer Joe to the new responsibilities of his less successful colleague, nor move Herb into Joe's position. What's in store for Joe is a big surprise. Joe's leader wants Joe to assume more responsibility and take over both industries! Joe's effective leader sees the mistake of placing Herb in Joe's slot. Why create a double risk? Joe might not succeed in his new position and Herb, who is less successful, might perform at his same lower level in Joe's position. A potential lose-lose.

Hence, the effective leader analyzes the responsibilities and the risks and rewards, and places Joe in charge of both areas, making Herb report to Joe.

Is this scenario really so uncommon? Isn't this what many effective leaders essentially do? They promote the best. They reward them by using their comfort zone as a springboard to growth. But this strategy does not assure success. Joe's leader needs to understand the stumbling blocks in the fields and valleys of Joe's world and help Joe to navigate through or around them. While Joe's colleague Herb may perceive this strategy as a demotion, the effective leader recognizes who is best left to remain in his comfort zone and who needs to move out. Not all chess pieces are castles or higher. Most are pawns, but a well-placed pawn can be an effective team member, and now and again capture the adversary or enemy.

So Joe's leader meets with him. But what does he tell him? What should he tell Joe as he unveils his strategy? Is it solely the proverbial "rah-rah" speech, or should it be more nuanced? Also, should Joe's leader also mention the change of responsibilities to Herb, or leave it to Joe to handle?

Let's analyze the two potential scenarios dealing with Joe. Scenario #1 is the rah-rah speech. Simply an acknowledgement of Joe's success and his colleague's underperformance and a big send-off to Joe as he is instructed to assume greater responsibility and, the scary concomitant, even greater results.

Scenario #2 is recognition of the difficult new fields and valleys Joe must cross while maintaining his level of success in the comfortable valley beyond which he is venturing. Many leaders might just bark the order to Joe. Of course, they don't perceive themselves as barking. They perceive their tone and words as a compliment and a wonderful challenge to Joe. Of course, it is! But the best leaders do much more. Why? Because they understand it's not the leader's perception that counts, it's Joe's perception that counts. Effective leaders acknowledge the interpersonal issues at all levels. They acknowledge the "new learn" Joe must undertake to understand the pharmaceutical industry. They acknowledge that Joe may think he will be spread too thin. But, then they explain to Joe why their faith and the faith of the organization is behind Joe. They support Joe's partial departure from his comfort zone. They know he can do it or he wouldn't have been chosen.

Joe should leave the meeting fearful, excited, and humble. He must now expand his leadership ability and the best way is by watching how his leader interacts with him and Herb, his less successful colleague. In this instance, almost every aspect of the initiative is positive. Herb may initially "swallow hard," but the effective leader explains that he is placing him in a more effective platform as Joe's number two in pharmaceuticals, maybe eventually also in information technology.

But a word more about the leader and Joe's less successful colleague. Nobody likes to deliver bad news. If Joe's leader is less than optimally effective, he may simply avoid Herb. What should he do? He should speak to Joe's colleague in a kind, honest, and firm manner and explain the growth path this change represents. In his heart, Herb knows he is coasting in his comfort zone. By speaking in an honest and positive manner to Herb, the effective leader gives Joe a heads-up to avoid sabotage. Joe will still have to enlist his colleague's loyalty and support. But why make it harder by a leader's silence?

The effective leader pulls Joe out of his comfort zone and attempts to expand the comfort zone of his colleague. As for the leader, he pulled himself out of his own comfort zone by re-staffing two critical areas of the company's business to solve an "okay performance" that he seeks to improve, while maintaining a good performance. If the initiative fails, Joe can return to his comfort zone duties. It will be the leader's failure. Leaders must risk failure all the time because the status quo of a corporate comfort zone suffocates all.

- Comfort zones represent the status quo. They are the antithesis of growth zones. Comfort zones eventually become stifling—they smother growth.
- Effective leaders seek to nudge subordinates from their comfort zones. They very best are always nudging themselves from their personal comfort zones.
- Effective leaders facilitate the acceptance of the new, of change. Effective leaders never take other's acceptance of change for granted. They embrace change and help others to do likewise.
- Effective leaders understand that all change is disruptive. They know it takes extra effort to walk the organization through the psychological and emotional mine fields of change.

CHAPTER 13

LEADERSHIP AND OVERLOAD (THE SALAMI APPROACH)

How often do we hear the phrase "one step at a time"? And, why has this trite and overused concept stood the test of time? The answer, of course, is that the concept is enduring and endearing in its simplicity and truth.

Effective leaders know that virtually any task, when isolated and focused upon, can be accomplished. They know that laser-like focus generally yields timely and satisfactory work. On the other hand, they understand that multi-tasking often yields inferior results.

While we often praise people who multi-task, do we understand exactly what we are praising? Not multi-tasking, *per se*. Effective leaders appreciate people who undertake more than one task at a time, but focus independently on each task so that all are well and timely completed.

Effective leaders understand that a subordinate may be responsible for completing multiple tasks simultaneously, and because they know multi-tasking, by definition, diffuses focus, they work to instill a sense of calm. Inner security allows us to believe enough in our ability to work on one task at a time, with full focus and concentration in the present working on the task at hand until it's finished or at a sensible break point before turning to another task or assignment.

Effective leaders understand that they must enable each of their subordinates to be as productive as their talent permits. They also understand that the less talented can often be equally effectual if they focus and concentrate. Leaders know that almost any subordinate can succeed if they reduce or remove distractions. Imagine if every employee treated each of his tasks as akin to walking across a room with a full-to-the-brim open jar of nitroglycerin. Imagine how much focus and concentration would be applied to complete that task!

Perhaps it's unrealistic to ask for or expect that level of focus. But why? Imagine the performance of each subordinate if that level of concentration were applied. Why shouldn't such focus be applied? So, you think it's human nature to try harder only when personal danger is the by-product of failure. You are right. Yet, effective leaders work to elevate a subordinate's focus by replacing the personal danger component with a positive desire to excel. To excel for themselves, to excel for their team, and to excel for their organization.

Effective leaders instill the pursuit of excellence. But how do they do it? What techniques do they use? Surely, a mere urging to pursue excellence cannot be the secret elixir. Of course, it isn't. Surely fear of danger—the danger of demotion or, worse, termination of employment—can't be the solution. Why not? Because the principle of negative incentive, the fear of failure, is just what it says. A negative! Capable leaders understand that fear is only effective so long as the fear is real and only for as long as it lasts. Sooner or later, the human psyche can no longer tolerate living with the fear. The result is the mind either rationalizes it away or buries it in the subconscious. Of course, the fear itself remains, even though it's mentally compartmentalized and stored away, it remains to erode confidence and self-esteem.

Fear is a short-term expedient that should only be used as a last resort, a final warning after which failure must yield termination. Only in that scenario is fear an appropriate device. It's a fair last-chance approach to enable a subordinate to dig deep within to synthesize the positive techniques previously taught but never mastered.

Great leaders preach self-development, growth, and confidence. They lead by example and teach subordinates how to read the signposts of success. Let's look at some tried and true leadership techniques.

Success begets success. Setting subordinates up for success, not failure, creates the foundation for further successes. Success will become a part of the fabric of a subordinate. Hence, effective leaders work hard to place subordinates in positions where success is within their grasp, but not assured. Smart leaders understand that by giving subordinates assignments that with a reach of effort they can handle, they are setting them up for success. Perhaps, the reach is initially small. That's okay. Any reach, by definition, is a reach. And a reach yielding a success registers in the psyche as a victory no matter how minimal the reach may be. Once the subordinate begins to believe in himself by having reached beyond his comfort zone successfully, more difficult tasks become doable. These slices of simple success create the foundation for larger successes by executing longer reaches. The "salami" in the salami approach comes in many varieties.

Sometimes the salami is an easy-reach task. Other times, it may be as simple as helping a subordinate prioritize tasks. Sometimes, however, it's more subtle—it's the leader who needs to understand that the salami is the subordinate who needs to be developed as an effective employee one slice at a time.

Let's assume the leader is starting an important project requiring an especially speedy and successful completion, but the only available employee isn't likely to get the job done on time. Less effective leaders will roll the dice and hope for the best. That's like going to a casino, and we all know the odds favor failure at every casino game. Smart leaders chart a critical path to success. Perhaps the leader himself will furnish the additional help, or develop a less-than-optimal but workable strategy to buy extra time for the subordinate to complete the project. There is virtually always an acceptable solution. Effective leaders abandon thoughts of perfection, which they know is a futile pursuit. The perfect 10 exists only in the movies (lucky Dudley Moore!). They know that 8s and 9s are often sufficient. They re-order their thinking to seek attainable results. Let's explore how it could work.

Assume a deadline is three days away and in an informal hallway chat the leader asks his subordinate how the task is progressing. The subordinate replies, "Okay." An ordinary leader might just accept that tepid response, but the effective leader will challenge it. It doesn't matter how important the task may be. What matters is the weak response. The leader follows up. "Will it be done on time?" And his subordinate says, "I think so. I think I can get it done by the deadline."

A leader might take that response as a yes. But was it? Of course not! Phrases like "okay," "I'll try," and "I think I can" are precursors to failure. They are permission slips for failure. The only acceptable response is a clear "I will." Phrases short of "I will" are requests to accept failure. Even worse, they are self-affirmations of likely failure—of failure as an acceptable outcome. Effective leaders must draw out the "I will" from their subordinates or drill down with questions to determine why the "I'll try" is the response. Understand their basis and find solutions to convert "I'll try" to "I will."

The words we speak reverberate back into our subconscious. In so doing, they either affirm our ability to move confidently forward to success or support our acceptance of potential failure. Failure sometimes happens. Even the best strike out from time to time. However, failure following a 100% effort is tolerable, even a learning experience—in humility, if nothing else.

Yet, allowing an internalization of failure by permitting words of failure to creep into our conversation is a failure far beyond the project that is put at risk. It is a failure of mind and spirit, which will eventually invade all tasks and even spread to other colleagues. From an *esprit de corps* perspective, the words are a precursor to a plague.

Effective leaders instill an "I will" culture. A culture which overcomes doubt and fear and allows each subordinate to believe in himself. A culture of reach. A culture that can grasp a new challenge. A culture that beckons employees to leave the safety of the comfort zone. A culture that breeds success, any success. A culture that allows each success to build a tidal wave washing onto the beaches of pursuit of excellence.

Let's look at another example of how effective leaders can create a culture which breeds success. How often has a leader asked a subordinate the "when" question? When will you write the memo? When will you meet with Mr. X? When will you start the assignment? When will you finish the project? Responses which contain the "if" qualifier are responses where failure is lurking, because a response containing an "if" is a conditional response. We all learned that "prepositional killer" in seventh or eighth grade English when we studied grammar. Effective leaders know that conditional responses are subject to external events. Perhaps if Mr. X takes my call, or if Mr. X agrees to meet, or if Joe, the colleague, completes his portion of the task, or any other event over which the subordinate does not have control. A seemingly legitimate condition, because the event requires the performance of a third party.

But effective leaders understand that successful employees will be secure enough to speak on an "if-less" basis. They may tell their leader that they need several preconditions to be met in order to complete their task, but they nevertheless convey an I-will attitude. Effective leaders drill down to understand the preconditions and assess whether their subordinate is realistically or unrealistically optimistic. If the optimism is rational, they find ways to support their subordinate. If the pessimistic ifs are irrational, they find ways to help their subordinate overcome their negativity.

Effective leaders balance rationality with a culture of success. In fact, there are circumstances where a failure might even be praised. A successful failure, so to speak, where the subordinate anticipated all the problems, addressed them, followed through, but nevertheless did not complete the task or completed it woefully late.

Effective leaders understand the concept of a successful failure. They understand the path to success is often littered with failure. Look to the baseball greats and see the Hall of Fame full of famous hitters who failed to hit safely 2 out of every 3 at-bats. Better yet, study the biography of virtually every famous scientist or inventor to see the mountain of failures preceding a simple success. Just consider Thomas Alva Edison, a man who failed over a thousand times before he succeeded and is credited with inventing the incandescent light bulb.

Good leadership occurs one conversation at a time, one constructive criticism at a time, and one compliment at a time. They know salami is best digested one slice at a time. Hence, when they wish to convey a criticism and a compliment, good leaders control the urge to combine them into one conversation. Effective leaders know that criticisms are noisy—absorbed quicker, and retained longer than compliments. They know that negative feedback affects the recipient more than twice as much as positive feedback, lingering in the mind long after the positive feedback has faded from memory. So, regardless of how busy they are, effective leaders find the time for two conversations, with the second being the complimentary one. Of course, constructive criticism is also a compliment when properly delivered. Nonetheless, most things, including salami slices, are best tackled, or digested, one slice at a time.

- Some leaders use fear to motivate. It's easy and it's lazy.
- Fear is a negative. True motivation stems from positivity. Success breeds success.
- Effective leaders seek to place subordinates on launching pads for success—not scaffolds of fear.
- Effective leaders work to remove phrases such as "I'll try," "I'll see," and "I think so." Rather, they seek to instill the organizational vocabulary with "I cans" and "I wills."
- Effective leaders avoid overloading subordinates with multiple projects. They help prioritize.
- Similarly, effective leaders work to avoid the "backwards compliment," or the so-called "mixed compliment."
- A negative compliment, no matter how cute, how "teasy," is a negative.
- A mixed compliment—a two-part comment with a negative and a positive, is remembered as a negative.
- Keep compliments clear and direct.
- Use another opportunity for the constructive criticism.

CHAPTER 14

LEADERSHIP AND THE LAWS OF CONDUCTIVITY AND CONNECTIVITY

Effective leaders are like automobile transmissions. They take the power of an idea or vision, like the engine power of a car, and transmit that power to the rear wheels. Effective leaders are the connectors-in-chief between a new idea or strategy and its implementation. They are also the conductors-in-chief between and among multiple offices and myriad employees. They understand that an initiative or strategy put into motion will remain in motion unless it meets resistance. Just as the friction points in a car create resistance, just as the heavy flywheel must go from a stationary position into motion, just as each wheel must begin to turn, so too must a leader overcome the obvious, the less than obvious (hidden), and the natural resistance of an organization in order to effect change.

Resistance exists in any medium. Whether it's the resistance we measure in ohms when calculating electrical conductivity or the resistance we feel as we propel ourselves in water. All efforts to create motion or continue in motion face resistance.

Likewise, when creating new directions or accelerating the speed of a current direction, resistance must be acknowledged and understood. Effective leaders know that virtually every change they seek to make will be met with some degree of resistance, regardless of the magnitude of the change. Why? Simply because most of us prefer things as they are. Perhaps Sir Isaac Newton expressed it best when he said, essentially, that things at rest tend to stay at rest. There is a comfort in the status quo. It's familiar and, for many, it's the way things are (read: "the way things should stay"). Hence, effective leaders understand that once they conceive a new initiative or strategy, they must then connect with their subordinates and achieve buy-in for their idea. Get the wheels rolling, so to speak. In other words, their most important sales job is to sell their idea to their staff. Now buy-in could be interpreted as the positive aspect of motivating the staff and, in fact, that's correct. But, that positive element will not be enough unless the buy-in is also employed to identify and neutralize the negative element, the resistance. It's surely two sides of the same coin, but each side deserves its due. In fact, buy-in cannot be consummated unless the leader addresses the positives of the new idea and overcomes the negatives associated with embracing change. Since risk is inherent in any change, the risk of failure must be acknowledged by the leader and then neutralized.

Because resistance can be pervasive and because it can be ever so insidious, effective leaders comb through the organization to uncover it. Once uncovered, it can be overcome. Resistance comes in so many forms, some unseen and unspoken. It can be a silent killer. Let's look at a few possible iterations.

Let's say Joe has been working in accounting for eleven years, all with the same system, and is now faced with an entirely new accounting program, technology he believes Sal, his peer, may be better equipped to master and use. Both Joe and Sal are vying for a promotion to director of accounting, a position that no doubt will be filled by one of them. How can the effective leader make both Joe and Sal feel an important part of the new project? Better yet, an integral part. How does an effective leader make each feel indispensable to the success of the new system? These are the challenges of the effective leader.

To unleash the full value of Joe and Sal, the effective leader needs to listen to each, not just listen with his ears and observe with his eyes, but listen with his whole being, listen with his heart. You might ask, "Why bother with Sal? He's the more likely to benefit." First of all, the effective leader may not yet know all of their relative strengths with respect to the new system. Second, there may be myriad sub-tasks that Joe can perform better than Sal even though Sal may be more proficient overall.

How does the effective leader communicate the new accounting initiative? Does the leader meet with the entire department and unveil the new program? Does the leader meet with Sal and Joe together? Does the leader meet with Sal and Joe separately? Yes. Effective leaders do all three presentations. Why? Because they want to succeed and they know that effective communication often requires more than one presentation. They know they need to invest the necessary time up front and build a foundation for success. Effective leaders know that a miscommunication can easily delay or even potentially derail a new initiative.

Hence, effective leaders clearly explain their vision, and make certain it is understood. In so doing, they can also find the hidden resistance to a new project. How? Simply by asking questions to confirm Sal or Joe's understanding of the initiative, thereby creating a "joinder" of vision between the leader and his subordinate, and then searching for the hidden landmines. Effective leaders unearth the landmines by asking questions. "What do you think?" "How long do you think the adoption process will take?" "Do you see any obstacles, staff-wise or otherwise?" And so on. Then, effective leaders listen to all of the responses, both verbal and non-verbal. Verbal responses come in the form of words, intonation, inflection, and tone. Non-verbal responses come in the form of body movement, whether as obvious as arms crossing and folding, or the other person's entire body pulling back, to as minimally detectable as a slight pursing of the lips, hard swallow, evasion of eye contact, tension or tautness in the face. Effective leaders intuitively understand the biometrics of voice and body movement. They pick up biomarkers, sometimes as subtle as an eye movement or the way and manner in which sentences are spoken, which reveal the true emotion. Effective leaders really look and listen, just as we were all taught as children before we ventured into traffic to cross the street.

Then, as employees respond to the leader's questions, the effective leader allows the subordinate to control the direction of the conversation, thereby allowing the subordinate to share ideas, consensus, and hidden fears. The effective leader doesn't just sell. He allows the subordinate to fill the leader's knowledge gaps so he can solve the hidden problems and overcome the hidden obstacles. Sometimes the subordinate's issues surface by his projecting his concerns and fears onto others. The effective leader listens with compassion, even empathy, and then finds ways to reinforce his vision and neutralize or deal with the concerns and fears that he allowed to bubble up.

Having met separately with Joe and Sal, the effective leader can then create a game plan for a combined meeting. He envisions the outcome he seeks and carefully weaves the tapestry of the joint meeting to produce the desired result. Then, the effective leader can either convene a departmental meeting or allow Joe or Sal or both to run that meeting.

You might be thinking, "Who has the time to do all of that?" Effective leaders always make the time necessary to at least start the engine, and in really difficult circumstances, even participate in the initial revolution of the flywheel.

Effective leaders understand that, except in special circumstances where knowledge alone is the end-product, knowledge only becomes truly valuable when it is combined with good judgment. Effective leaders create a Petri dish for each subordinate to incubate and produce his genius. That sticky goo of each subordinate's knowledge and good judgment that when combined thickens the agar of a positive *esprit de corps*.

By truly trying to understand each employee's needs and desires, by really listening and trying to really get it, effective leaders develop a trust with their subordinates. A real connection. And once the connection is made, the wheels start to turn. But how can an effective leader spend enough time, invest enough focus, to develop a connection with each subordinate? Unless it's a small organization, it's probably impractical, if not impossible.

Effective leaders must develop the leadership abilities of their captains. Just as an admiral is charged with commanding the fleet, each captain is charged with commanding his ship or boat. Each captain becomes an extended connector, translating and interpreting the leader's vision so the troops in the field can execute the plan or strategy. These linchpin employees, the leader's captains, lieutenants, and sergeants, are the chain of command through which the leader's energy and passion flow. How else could an admiral or any other leader command his fleet?

But, there's more. Not only must the effective leader impart positivity and neutralize resistance, he must also avoid destructive outbursts. The outbursts of his subordinates or, worse, himself! Whether it's a vendor who delivered a shipment late or a competitor who used some unfair or unethical advantage, effective leaders know that attacking the other person is not nearly as effective as embracing a positive solution. Effective leaders know that negative comments, attacks of any kind, will most likely only impair the object of the attack temporarily, if at all, and can never create a foundation of growth for the attacker. Why?

When we attack another we are seeking, hoping for, a negative result. Or, to put it somewhat mathematically, when we seek a result (a positive), but the result we seek is negative (a negative), we create an overall negative. It's simple math. Plus 1 multiplied by minus 1 equals minus 1 ($+1 \times -1 = -1$). Effective leaders understand that, even worse, by hoping for a negative result, we lessen or remove our focus from our positive efforts. We subliminally let down our optimistic and positive guard. Once we allow that to occur, negativity bleeds into us and we risk becoming negative. As Thoreau pointed out, to paraphrase liberally, eventually we become our dominant thoughts.

Effective leaders understand they are conductors. They are, simultaneously, conductors of their organizational orchestra, and conductors of their vision to each musician, each employee, constituting the orchestral organization.

Even more so, effective leaders are responsible for the connection among all subordinates. They are responsible, whether through their captains and others or directly, to maintain not only conductivity but also connectivity. Conductivity is only at its most effective with connectivity.

As the saying from Verizon urges us to remember, "We're all connected." Effective leaders understand the laws of conductivity, but the very best strive for constant connectivity. They spend the time necessary with Joe and Sal. They know there is a structural jealousy which creates resistance that they want to ameliorate. Effective leaders conduct just like the leaders of an orchestra. And they know that maximum performance requires a united sound, a united *esprit de corps*, synthesized from the positive connections between and among each player. We may be all connected, as the advertisement states, but effective leaders understand that conductivity and connectivity are his dual charges.

- Effective leaders are orchestra conductors—they seek to connect each member to create harmony with the other members and with the organization's goals.
- Effective leaders blend all of the instruments of the company into a single harmonized melody. They seek to conduct and connect.
- Effective leaders don't use a trumpet when an E-flat clarinet is required. At worst, they substitute a different woodwind.
- Effective leaders acknowledge and accept resistance to change, resistance to new ideas. They do not resent it. They understand it's natural and that change reflects the unknown which most fear on some level.
- Effective leaders work hard to lead others into the unknown and to expressly or impliedly send the message that the next unknown will be a new safe harbor, a better comfort zone (at least for a while).
- Effective leaders understand the counterintuitivity of controlling the direction of a meeting by asking questions, carefully listening, and then asking further questions. Never interrupting, never judging.

- The best leaders continually seek to fill their knowledge gaps. They always seek to be early knowers.
- Effective leaders make the time necessary to get into the field. They know it's too difficult to conduct and connect from the corner office. They keep the famous adage of General Electric near the forefront of their mind, "people are our most important product."

Chapter 15

LEADERSHIP AND FACE

Effective leaders save face, but not in the traditional sense of the expression. Saving face, in the normal sense, is a sign of poor or ineffective leadership. Therefore, the effective leader never seeks to save face. On the other hand, ineffective leaders save face by blaming subordinates or otherwise. It is a form of shifting responsibility for failure. Effective leaders accept adversity, changed circumstances, and unforeseen risks and challenges. They embrace setbacks by perceiving them as opportunities to solve problems and overcome submerged obstacles.

It is the literal face effective leaders save. The physical facial expression—theirs and those of their subordinates. They save that face by studying the facial expressions of others, and learning to control their own facial expressions as well. Let's consider an all-too-common circumstance, and explore the impact of two very different facial expressions.

Let's assume a leader's subordinate reports to his superior in their weekly meeting. He reports that a new competitor has not only entered the market but is quickly gaining market share, perhaps because of better pricing or an apparently more effective product. The subordinate is upset to have to report this information and is highly concerned, even fearful. He is highly concerned for the company and perhaps fearful of his leader's reaction.

What must the effective leader do? How should she respond? Would it make sense to show surprise? Would anger or frustration be an appropriate response? Should the leader complain about not learning about this competitor sooner? Does any response that could be interpreted as fearful by the subordinate make sense? Will any response indicating surprise or concern convey the kind of message a leader wants to deliver to his subordinate? Should the leader show any of these faces? Of course not!

Effective leaders understand the aphorism "Never let them see you sweat." They understand they are the rudder of the corporate ship. They cannot tolerate wobble, and actions which could be perceived by their subordinates as wobble must be immediately stabilized.

New information comes in a variety of ways. Sometimes by surprise. But effective leaders understand that surprises are normal. Surprises lurk in every existing initiative and often congregate in new initiatives. Effective leaders understand that surprises are not surprises at all. A surprise is simply a new fact or a bundle of new information arriving in a disjointed time sequence. Hence, effective leaders respond to surprise with equanimity. They remain calm and collected. They control their emotions. They accept the new reality and absorb it so they can develop an effective response.

They respond, "That's good input," or "Let's see if we can dig into this deeper so we can formulate an action plan," or "Glad you told me now and didn't wait to first find out more." They never demean the messenger.

Effective leaders understand that change itself is the constant. Their task is not to view change just as a challenge but as an opportunity to revisit their strategy and tactics and improve upon both.

Perhaps most important, they know their subordinate will remember their reaction—their leader's "face"—the expression of his leader when he reported the negative input. Will the subordinate remember his leader's face of fear or of calmness, assuredness, and positivity?

Whether we realize it or not, we all study facial expressions. We all save the face of others as they react in stressful situations, just as others will save ours. We inherited this ability from our animal ancestors. For them it was a matter of survival. Could a low crouched wildcat with ears laid back against his head be mistaken for other than a stalking verge-of-attack posture? Effective leaders understand the impact of their facial expression. Effective leaders just don't react to oral responses. They react to the whole person, words, intonation, cadence, inflection, and body movement. Often the most important "tell" derives from body language. Body language can disclose true feelings and reactions, and the most frequent of those movements are often changes in facial expression.

Facial expressions can say so much. The science of reading facial expressions has given rise to facial recognition technology, just as the science of audio recognition uses sophisticated audio recognition technology. Imagine if the manufacturer of a household canned good, like baked beans, could monitor the initial facial reaction of a supermarket shopper upon first glance at his product versus their first glance at the beans of a competitor. Imagine if a camera could record the facial expression of theatergoers as the feature film was being screened, or television audiences as they view various scenes in a sitcom, or different commercials.

Wouldn't it be revealing to know if the reaction sought from a particular scene or advertisement was the reaction actually felt by the audience? Wouldn't it be valuable to know if the reactions to a movie or advertisement were in sync with or divergent from the desired or expected reaction? Facial recognition technology will provide that feedback. Similarly, audio recognition technology may soon be able to interpret an emotional state without analyzing words, but just from tone, pitch, and intonation.

We communicate so much with and through our face. It's no surprise that effective leaders understand that subordinates read their leader's face and mentally store a visual imprint of what their leader is really saying and feeling. Once stored, that visual imprint becomes the non-verbal recollection of what they heard and saw—ironically, regardless of what they were actually hearing and seeing.

That doesn't mean leaders should be stone-faced all of the time. To the contrary, leaders use their facial expressions to help them communicate, as do we all. However, it does mean that, more often than not, a leader should be stone-faced upon receipt of unsettling news. Why? A composed reaction says "Tell me more" or "I'm pleased you told me" all in a non-judgmental manner. Leaders need information. Effective leaders are early knowers. Poor leaders learn critical information woefully late, or never at all. Effective leaders allow their subordinates to bleed information and help them drain it all out. They know it's hard for an associate or subordinate to deliver bad news to a superior. Subordinates have self-clotting techniques that may prevent them from remembering, much less disclosing, all the unpleasant facts they know. Effective leaders avoid the self-defeating clotting techniques described in Chapter 1. Equally important, they practice to avoid the facial expressions that can clot a conversation. Coagulation is easy enough for a subordinate delivering "bad news" without the leader adding a dose of Vitamin K.

Delivering bad news is like giving blood. There is often a pre-donation anxiety. But, oh, the gratification after it's over! Effective leaders understand the pre-meeting anxiety. They, too, want, in a sense, to make the meeting unemotional, thereby allowing the subordinate to keep giving information. The leader patiently allows the process to unfold with as many facts as the subordinate can remember on his own, and by prodding with non-demeaning questions to help the subordinate recall facts otherwise considered unimportant or insignificant.

We all carry a valise full of facial expressions. Most expressions evaporate like the morning dew, but sometimes our expressions are imprinted on another, perhaps more often than we would like to think.

Certainly, saving the face of another in a mental image is something we all do at least some of the time. So, make sure it's the face you want saved!

- Communication is effected aurally and visually. It requires all of our senses.
- Most of us can "watch our words." Yet, we are too often betrayed by our facial expressions and body movements.
- Effective leaders know they must neutralize any visuals as a result of facial expressions or hand or body movement—visuals that show disdain or a reaction other than what they should convey.
- Effective leaders seek to respond neutrally to new ideas, new thoughts, and, most of all, unpleasant surprises. Imagine the general of an army who learns the enemy is much closer and better positioned than he thought. What would his "captains and lieutenants" think if the general responded with either words or a facial expression that said or expressed, "Oh, my goodness, what am I going to do."
- Effective leaders always want to know and learn more. When surprised they respond, "tell me more."

CHAPTER 16

LEADERSHIP FOR LAWYERS AND LITIGANTS—PART I

Like it or not, leaders will most likely be consumers of litigation services or, if lawyers, providers of litigation services. Since litigation has become pervasive in our society, with little chance that any organization will always avoid it, the following offers advice and guidance on how to use litigation more effectively.

It is a misconception that litigation is the antithesis of negotiation; that negotiation is the use of compromise in order to reach agreement, while litigation is a zero sum game with a winner and a loser; that litigation disregards the concept of compromise; in theory, when compromise cannot be reached, litigation ensues. Litigation is just like war. Just as war was famously described by Carl von Clausewitz as ". . . politics by other means," litigation is negotiation by other means. But litigation is not just about war; litigation should be viewed as the continuation of negotiations, intensified and complicated by complaints, motions, depositions, and other weapons in the arsenal of litigators.

Ironically, when it comes to litigation, corporations may find themselves as inexperienced and ill-prepared as individuals. Lawsuits involving corporations are almost always commercial in nature, involving disputes over money. Perhaps the most common type of commercial litigation is a suit to recover an amount owed by one company to another, usually in connection with the sale of a product or service. Let's assume you are either corporate counsel or outside counsel for a corporation.

Much civil litigation is conducted before a presiding judge, rather than a jury. As a result, litigation, in a sense, involves three parties. You, your adversary, and the judge. Hence, it makes sense to understand this tri-party dynamic. Of course, the judge isn't technically a party in the suit, but the judge is critical to the outcome. Why? Because if you fail to settle the suit before trial, you must focus on facilitating the judge's understanding of your side and recognition that your position should prevail.

You need to develop approaches to make it easier for the judge to understand and agree with your position. You want to make the judge feel comfortable and "right" in finding for your client. Judges are people, too—they have families. They may have a problem child. They may be buying a new house. They may be fighting with their contractor over remodeling the kitchen. They may be fighting with a neighbor because the neighbor's kid has a noisy garage band. In other words, judges enjoy and suffer from all the joys, fulfillment, and trespasses that we do, so we need to be sensitive to their humanity, and understand the tolls on their professional and personal life.

The judge's interest in the outcome of your lawsuit may be minimal. Not only might the case be insignificant from the judge's perspective, no matter how important we think the matter is, but it may be insignificant in relation to the other commercial, even criminal, cases that the judge must decide. Let's face it—regardless of the outcome, the world will go on. Most likely no one will really care except the parties to the litigation. So, how do we get the judge to empathize with our position?

If you are in-house counsel, your lawyer may advise you that you have a good case because the law is on your side. That's a good thing, but it may not be enough, particularly if the strength of your case is based on a technical point. More often than not, the facts determine on whose side the victory gavel will fall. It is the equities of the case, the more compelling facts, that generally determine the victor. It is seldom esoteric technical legal points that win cases. Isn't that the way it ought to be?

Therefore, to litigate most effectively, put yourself in the position of the judge. In so doing, you can understand how the judge might react. Isn't it likely the judge will want to lean toward the side with the greater equity—the side whose facts make a decision in its favor seem to be the fairer result? To determine if your position is compelling, ask yourself, "How would the judge's spouse respond if the facts of your case were described over dinner?" Would she think you had the more equitable position? Would she feel compelled to suggest that the fairer and better result is for you to win? If you believe judges are just like us, and I assure you they are, then you must also assume that judges will seek to find for the party with the greater equities. Your job (or your attorney's) is to determine how to best present your case so that it cries out for the judge to find in your favor. Are your facts clear and compelling, or can they be construed in several ways? Put yourself in your adversary's shoes. Put yourself in the judge's shoes. That's an important part of preparation. You must try to understand the varying perspectives. You may not agree with them. You may think they are outrageous (that's your ego rising). But you must understand them. Allow yourself to see the other side's equities by lifting the blinders that your ego creates. Then you will more effectively present your position.

The problem with litigators is they spend too much time litigating. Of course, that is what they are trained to do. They are trained to attack and counterattack. They use motions and briefs to win battles. They are good at it. But, remember, it's the war, not the battle, that must be won. Moreover, litigators are not business people. They have honed their skills as litigation lawyers, so their mindset may not always be in sync with you, their client. Not because they don't care, not because they don't want to win, but because they may want to win too much. They may be focusing solely on winning. You may (rightly) see the litigation as an additional negotiating tool to reach a business result, as additional leverage to resolve the aborted negotiations. Wise clients (and their attorneys) seek to find inflection points in the litigation process where their negotiating leverage has increased. Then, they often seek to settle advantageously. It is not easy to litigate to conclusion. It's time-consuming and expensive. Fewer than 10% of all cases come to a trial and final verdict. In fact, very few cases go all the way. They shouldn't! The reasons are business-oriented and practical. There is always a risk of loss at trial. Moreover, it is generally preferable for the clients to control the outcome of the litigation via settlement. They are closest to and most knowledgeable about the dispute. Aren't they really in the best position to reach the best settlement? If the parties are struggling to reach settlement, most judges will (in varying ways and to varying degrees) pressure both sides to settle anyway. Judges know how time-consuming and costly a trial can be. Court calendars are full. Judges are pressed by their superiors—yes, judges have bosses, too—to clear their calendars. They want to move cases as quickly as reasonably possible.

As individuals, our litigation is personal to us. Most of our contact with litigation is matrimonial or related to accidents and insurance. We tend to become emotional, and therefore, we tend to allow ego to blind us. We confuse ego with the concept of principle. Hence, in the name of principle, we look to the court system for revenge, to make sure we are not taken advantage of, or to prove we are right. Our ego will not allow us to accept that the divorce, the auto accident—whatever—was, at least in part, our fault. Isn't it ironic how quickly we convince ourselves it's the other guy's fault? How often have we heard, "It's not about the money, it's about the principle"? Well, it's neither about the money nor the principle. Usually, it's about the ego. Eventually, we learn the court system is not a modern-day version of a torture chamber. It's not going to exact justice in the manner we wish. It is not going to grant revenge. In fact, we may not even obtain what we think is fair. Rather, after a slow, expensive, cumbersome process, we either settle or have the judgment of a dispassionate third party (the judge) settle the matter for us.

Matrimonial litigation is probably the type most of us will encounter on a personal level, so it requires a few words. Because divorce is so personal, it is fraught with emotion. It is fertile for ego. It is fertile for outrage. However, ego and outrage are our enemies. If allowed to surface, they will urge us to draw blood, to use the judicial system to hurt the person we once loved. The judicial system, however, cannot and will not participate in revenge.

Ego and outrage will accomplish only two results. They increase the length of the litigation and therefore the cost to both parties, and they force both parties to maintain their focus on the litigation. Both parties remain chained to the past longer, so neither is able to move forward. The irony of matrimonial litigation (if there is no dispute over custody)—as is the case with most litigation involving money—is that the settlement the parties agree to is usually within 10%, plus or minus, of what a judge might order after a full trial. It's tough, but even in matrimonial litigation the wise party buries ego and dissipates rage. Aren't these concepts applicable in commercial litigation?

How can we deal more effectively with our litigation? Let's consider corporate in-house counsel seeking to identify outside counsel to represent the corporation. Assume in-house counsel has many friends working for other corporations, and has obtained a list of recommended law firms. How might in-house counsel select litigation counsel? What are the road rules for purchasing a litigator?

Road Rule #1: Find the right door to enter into the law firm. In other words, is in-house counsel entering through a powerful attorney or a lower-level friend? Of course, it should not make a difference, and in fact, it may not. However, a powerful partner will likely be more effective in marshalling the best the law firm has to offer. It's common sense that a law firm with many litigators cannot have hired all A+ quality attorneys. No one hires quite that well. Therefore, it's simply more likely that a more powerful attorney will be able to deliver the firm's top guns or simply assemble the most cost-effective team. Generally, proper staffing trumps billable rates.

Road Rule #2: Make sure that in-house counsel can be sure the litigation will be conducted cost-effectively. This is the cost-benefit matrix. Will litigation be more expensive than the potential settlement amount? Someone at the law firm must track the litigation costs.

Settlement opportunities arise as frequently as the litigator can create appropriate circumstances, and include the proverbial "on the doorsteps before trial" or even much earlier, at the beginning or conclusion of an important deposition, or by virtue of unintended meetings between adversaries. Moreover, settlement opportunities will be created by the court, whether via mandatory mediation or otherwise. Remember, litigators like to litigate. However, blind litigation, with an attitude of "full speed ahead—take no prisoners" is simply not cost effective, except in the rarest of circumstances.

Litigation is negotiation by other means. It's negotiation, pressure-elevated by virtue of the cost and time of litigation and the risk of loss. These pressures have an impact on both parties, which often facilitates settlement. Settlement almost always makes sense. Reasonable (non-ego-filled) clients are the most suited to resolve a dispute. They are the most knowledgeable and interested in their matter, certainly more than a third-party arbitrator or judge.

- Effective leaders understand that litigation is a sophisticated tool to effect a business result.
- They remove their ego from the conflict—they do not invest themselves in the litigation. If it's not a "bet-the-ranch" case, then it's just business.
- They seek to understand all sides of the conflict—all three!
- Effective leaders understand that compelling facts can trump the law in a variety of scenarios, and most everything trumps technical niceties.
- Effective leaders understand litigation is an inefficient tool. Hence, they continually think of litigation in a cost-benefit matrix context in order to seek advantageous opportunities to settle.
- Effective leaders recognize that most litigation is not about principle, it's about principal!
- Effective leaders understand a win does not require victory. Strategic retreats can be as or more effective than the cost of victory.

Chapter 17

LEADERSHIP FOR LAWYERS AND LITIGANTS—PART II

Have you ever been disappointed in both the litigation system and your attorney? Perhaps you felt the result was not right, that it fell below even your reduced expectations. That's due to ego. The litigation "fire" is fed by the ego of one or both of the parties, one or both of whom need to be right, need to prove to themselves, to their boss, to the world, that they are right. Remove the ego and focus on solving the problem. Listen to what the other side is saying. Stop having to be right! Stop selling your position as the only viable one. Then you may be able to find a solution. If the solution causes settlement, you've saved money, and the often greater expense of continuing to deal with the past, inhibiting you from focusing on a positive, forward-looking personal or corporate agenda.

Ironically, the client—you—may have your ego under control. Your lawyer may be insisting on being right—on winning, no matter what. It's somewhat analogous to going to a cardiologist versus a cardiac surgeon. Generally, the cardiologist will seek to solve the problem through medication; on the other hand, the surgeon will suggest solving the problem through surgery. Cardiologists are taught to cure with medication, while surgeons are taught to cure with surgery. So, too, transactional lawyers are taught to cure by negotiating to settlement; litigators are taught to cure by litigating to victory. We, as clients, must control the litigation, just as we, as patients, must make the final decision regarding our medical care. No one knows the facts of our legal case better than we do, just as no one knows how our body feels better than we do. We simply need to remove our blinders to understand all perspectives.

Perhaps our litigation is inexorably moving toward the trial stage. Despite our efforts, the case isn't settling. It certainly takes two to make a deal. No matter how good a negotiator we may be, it may not be possible to settle the matter. Chances are the dispute causing the litigation started with an exchange of correspondence. Perhaps the parrying began months or even years ago. Perhaps each felt the other side's position was 100% wrong. Remember the lifespan of written words. They never go away!

They will be produced as part of the discovery process in any litigation. E-mails are forever, too, so treat them as formal letters. Write them with clarity, without rage or emotion. Less is more. Don't say too much, and don't allow yourself to say things you wish you could retract. Don't stake out or lock yourself into positions before you have all the facts.

Once litigation begins, there will be correspondence (whether via e-mail or letter), complaints, briefs, motions, and replies. A judge's clerk will be reading these papers. Perhaps the clerk is 26 years old. Perhaps the judge will ask for the clerk's opinion of each side's equities. Like it or not, the judge may never read all the papers. The judge may only read the first several pages of each brief. Hence, while all of your papers should be terrific, give particular focus to the preliminary statements. Is your position compelling without reading on? Is it clear and convincing without reading on? Does it have a ring of authenticity and legitimacy that will resonate in the clerk's or the judge's stomach? Will the judge want to find for you and support your position, without reading on? If not, rewrite it. Rewrite your papers until they are compelling. Adverbs and adjectives won't strengthen your position or weaken the other side's. Inflammatory words that demean the other side will not help. You may wish to insert emotion. But, remember, others will only read the words on the page. The judge must be dispassionate and impartial. The judge has seen and heard it all before. Clerks and judges will look past the noise. They will focus on the facts to determine the equities. Emotional attacks do not resonate with the impartial trier of fact. What resonates is a clear and compelling exposition of the facts—facts that, were you to read them without technical niceties, without nuance and devoid of spin, make your position compelling, notwithstanding appropriate credence to the position of the other side.

To write convincingly requires the removal of ego. Remember the bromide that there are three sides to every story—your side, your adversary's, and the truth or perspective that falls somewhere in between. Have you presented an honest and compelling story of your facts? Is it readable? Is it digestible? Will it resonate with the sympathies of the clerk and/or the judge? If their spouses heard your story, would they say that your position is better and you should prevail? It may seem disingenuous to think litigation should be analyzed in such manner, but it is useful.

Road Rule #3 requires a recognition that even the best litigators can become caught up in the moment. They may react poorly to attacks on their client or themselves. Do not let that happen (control ego). It is expensive and unproductive. It will only create more paper, more expense, and further separation between the parties. It will cause the parties to become more invested in their position. They will become more centered on proving they are right rather than listening to the other side. Thoughts of finding an appropriate and cost-effective compromise will evaporate. Some cases need to go all the way. However, the chances are that the case in which you are involved should be settled.

Perhaps you are the attorney. You are about to appear before the court. Perhaps it's your very first court appearance. Perhaps you have been asked to handle a small part of the case for a senior partner. Would it be inappropriate for you to approach the judge (approach the bench) with your adversary, and indicate you are inexperienced? This is a technique of humanizing the relationship between you and the judge. Perhaps you think it inappropriate to make such a statement. Why, if it's true? By the same token, when you begin your presentation focus on the judge and the judge's facial expressions. Use that feedback to adjust your comments. Don't proceed blindly. Oftentimes, judges will interrupt and take control. This might fluster you. Instead, consider yourself lucky, consider it a look into the judge's perception of the case. Good trial lawyers would rather be interrupted to be able to better respond to the judge's real concerns. As you present your argument, observe the judge's reaction for clues to help you adjust your direction and emphasis. On the other hand, you may have to ad-lib when the judge poses a question you are not sure you can properly answer. Don't be afraid to humbly ask the judge to clarify the question. This will provide the opportunity to catch your breath. Perhaps the judge will give you more insight by rephrasing the question or just elaborating further. Listen carefully; absorb the words and the silence between the words. Wait until you hear the silent period when the judge finishes. Reflect for a few seconds before responding. Remember, sometimes the answer is embedded in the question. Listen with all of your senses. Use your eyes, ears, and heart—all of your senses.

As you are presenting your argument or your client's testimony, you might be interrupted by your adversary. The adversary may object to something you said. That objection may, or may not, be perceived by the Court as appropriate. Don't talk over your adversary. Listen to what he is saying. It's seldom wise to jump in. Give the judge a chance to react. You'll get your chance to respond, or perhaps the judge will tell your adversary to sit down. The more experience in court, the better you will be able to absorb all that is occurring in the courtroom while you speak. Is your adversary fidgeting, or sitting calmly? Is the judge making faces? Do you sense the judge wants to interrupt yet is holding back as you press on? What should you do?

Practice developing all your senses. If you think you are not being persuasive, and you feel the judge is about to interrupt, stop and allow the silence to be filled with a comment by the judge. On the other hand, if you feel you are hitting pay dirt, press forward. You need to learn to take in all the vibrations emanating from the judge—perhaps even from the judge's clerk—and, of course, from your adversary. It will help you determine your direction and emphasis, and when to allow yourself to be interrupted. All of this will develop with experience. But all the experience in the world will not be enough if you haven't learned to observe while you speak.

So how can you speak and listen with all of your senses as you make your presentation? By being fully prepared. If you are prepared, as you present your case you will pick up the vibrations of your adversary and the judge. What you have to say and how you present it may not change the outcome of the case. However, it is more likely that if you present yourself in a calm and knowledgeable way, the judge will be able to better listen to what you are saying and fully absorb your words. You don't want to undercut the judge's understanding with distracting emotion, and don't expect the judge to support your client simply because you are more likeable. However, you can assume the judge will be able to better listen to what you are saying if you present your arguments with grace. The reality is that we all pay more attention to those who make us comfortable, as opposed to those who attack. Raising your voice will not make your words more convincing. Don't use invective, and don't go off on tirades. Those antics simply stir up tempers. It becomes more difficult for the judge to listen to you. Sound negotiating techniques will allow the judge to listen to what you are saying and better understand your position—your equities.

If litigation is just another form of negotiation, why should the parties have to litigate any garden-variety commercial dispute? Because one or both parties cannot remove themselves from their need to be right. If you sense this in the other side, use their intractability to your advantage. Find a way to present your papers and your oral arguments to put forth your position in a compelling and equitable manner; yet, at the same time, focus on pressure points to cause your adversary to further emotionalize his position. Then, your adversary may make unintended and ill-considered comments. The same concepts that apply to a negotiation apply to litigation. Pressure or rage can squeeze us to let something slip out that we wish we could take back.

Don't allow your ego to blind you from seeing your adversary's position. Don't allow your ego demand to win every single point, regardless of its significance. In virtually all matters, litigation or otherwise, there are usually just a few (sometimes only one) core facts. Technical legal points and secondary and tertiary facts seldom, if ever, have an impact on a result. If you are the client, it's your job to be a smart client. If you are the attorney, it's your absolute obligation to understand the core facts and principles. Then, it's your job to present them in a manner to compel the judge to find for your client by appealing to equity and fairness. It's virtually impossible to see the key elements of your case when you are fixated on being right on every issue. To really understand the core issues, you must understand the other side's position and needs—the second position—regardless of what you think of them; but to be fully effective you must accept and understand the reality of a third position. You'll find it if you take the time to free-think the theory of the case. Listen to the feedback from those with whom you discuss the case, regardless of their reaction, and don't disregard it, no matter how surprising you may find it. To make your best presentation you need to see all sides. What's the point in making a great argument about 17 minor points, if you fail to convince the clerk or the judge on the core issue—the fulcrum of the case? Work on getting to the heart. The broken limb must be mended; cuts will heal themselves. Make sure you see and understand the issues that go to the heart of the matter. The jugular issues are the only ones that get directly to the heart of the matter.

- Effective leaders work hard to keep their ego and that of their legal team in check.
- Litigation is just business—there is no place for ego, outburst or rage.
- Good leaders do not allow their attorneys to overwork a matter or fight to the death.
- Effective leaders seek counsel who understand their business and never lose sight of the goal in most litigations—achieve a settlement as advantageous as possible, given the facts, in relationship not to the money spent, but in relationship to the money and time yet to be spent.
- Effective leaders understand litigation requires the litigants to "look backward," diverting their focus and attention. They know success requires a "looking forward" perspective with concentration on new ideas and initiatives.

AFTERWORD

Effective leaders are effective in all they undertake, whether in the corporate board room, the corporate field, the courtroom, the negotiating table or the dinner table! They are just as effective with their friends, colleagues and, most important, loved ones. Why? Because the attributes identified with effective leaders transcend the business world and permeate all aspects of life. Effective leaders know they make mistakes, they don't always get things right on the first try, and sometimes they allow their ego to "escape" and momentarily get the better of them. Yet, by acknowledging mistakes and correcting them, by "trying harder" (just like the old Avis commercial) and by vigilant management of their ego, the goal they seek to attain is effectiveness.

Is the ability to really listen to the other person any different in the context of boss-employee relationship than in the context of parent-child relationship? Are the necessary skills set out at the end of the last chapter any less important when dealing with your teenager than when dealing with your litigation or business adversary?

How often does our spouse or our child interrupt us when we are working on our car, working on a home improvement, watching a riveting movie or a tension-filled sporting event? Do we stop what we are doing and really listen to what is being said? Aren't these interactions the negotiations and deals that count the most? Perhaps a spouse asking about a future vacation, a party you both are planning, or a child seeking permission to use the family car, stay out late, go abroad for the summer—or just permission to get your attention! Leadership comes in many varieties. Make sure all "57" are equally effective.

The elements of effective leadership make us much more than effective leaders. They allow us to become more effective human beings.